D0458374

TRACTION

TRACTION

How Any Startup Can Achieve
Explosive Customer Growth

GABRIEL WEINBERG
and JUSTIN MARES

Portfolio / Penguin

PORTFOLIO / PENGUIN
An imprint of Penguin Random House LLC
375 Hudson Street
New York, New York 10014
penguin.com

Copyright © 2015 by Gabriel Weinberg and Justin Mares
Penguin supports copyright. Copyright fuels creativity, encourages diverse voices, promotes free speech, and creates a vibrant culture. Thank you for buying an authorized edition of this book and for complying with copyright laws by not reproducing, scanning, or distributing any part of it in any form without permission. You are supporting writers and allowing Penguin to continue to publish books for every reader.

ISBN 978-1-59184-836-3

Printed in the United States of America
1   3   5   7   9   10   8   6   4   2

Set in Adobe Caslon Pro
Designed by Spring Hoteling

While the author has made every effort to provide accurate telephone numbers, Internet addresses, and other contact information at the time of publication, neither the publisher nor the author assumes any responsibility for errors or for changes that occur after publication. Further, the publisher does not have any control over and does not assume any responsibility for author or third-party Web sites or their content.

CONTENTS

CONTENTS

CONTENTS

Preface: Traction Trumps Everything

In 2006 I sold for millions of dollars an Internet company that I had cofounded a few years earlier. It was a strange company for many reasons, not the least of which was that we had no employees from beginning to end. I wrote every line of code and did all the accounting and customer support.

The terms of the deal were such that my cofounder and I didn't have to work for the acquiring company at all. We were free to move on to other things, and we did. A few months later my wife and I moved from our 865-square-foot apartment near Boston to a country house twenty-five miles outside of Philadelphia. I had just turned twenty-seven.

She went to her job and I sat at home doing nothing for the first time in my life. We knew no one for a hundred miles in any direction.

Naturally, I started tinkering on the computer again, starting about a dozen side projects simultaneously. A year and a half later, I thought I was on to something. I noticed two things that bothered me about Google: too much spam (all those sites with nothing but ads) and not enough instant answers (I kept going to Wikipedia and IMDb). I thought if I could easily pick out the spam and the answers, then I'd have a more compelling search engine.

Both problems were harder to solve than I initially thought, but I thoroughly enjoyed the work and kept at it. Everyone I talked to about my search engine project thought I was nuts. You're doing what? Competing against Google? Why? How? Another year later, in the fall of 2008, I flipped the switch, unveiling my search engine to the public.

DuckDuckGo had a rather uneventful launch, if you can even call it a launch. I posted it to a niche tech site called *Hacker News* and that was the long and short of it. The post was entitled "What do you think of my new search engine?"

Like many entrepreneurs, I'm motivated by being on the cusp of something big, and I was at the point where I needed some validation. I can survive on little, but I needed something.

I got it.

Granted, the product wasn't anything you'd want to switch to at that point, and people let me know that. It was an Internet forum, after all. However, I still felt there was genuine interest in a new search competitor. I could tell some people were growing wary of what Google was becoming. For example, those initial conversations led me to investigate search privacy and eventually become "the search engine that doesn't track you," years before government and corporate surveillance became a mainstream issue.

In any case, the response I received was enough motivation to keep me going. Which brings me to traction. I needed some.

Traction is the best way to improve your chances of startup success. Traction is a sign that something is working. If you charge for your product, it means customers are buying. If your product is free, it's a growing user base.

Traction is powerful. Technical, market, and team risks are easier to address with traction. Fund-raising, hiring, press, partnerships, and acquisitions all become much easier.

In other words, *traction trumps everything*.

My last startup had grown using two traction channels: first, search engine optimization (ranking high in search engines for relevant terms), and later, viral marketing (where your customers bring in other customers, such as by referring friends and family through use of the product).

Viral marketing doesn't work well in search because you can't easily bake it into the product by putting stuff between people and their search results. So I tried search engine optimization. The terms "search engine" and "search engines" were too hard to rank for, as the high-ranking companies had been around for a decade and had tens of thousands of links pointing at them from their long histories. "New search engine" was more in my grasp.

I worked hard for many months to rank high for this phrase. The key to good search engine optimization (SEO) is getting links. As you will read later in the SEO chapter, you need a strategy to get these links in a scalable way.

Getting stories written about you in blogs and news outlets is a common SEO linking strategy. However, I hit saturation with that channel strategy pretty quickly and it didn't get me to the top. Something more creative was required.

After much brainstorming and experimenting, I eventually hit upon a good idea. I built a karma widget that would display links to your social media profiles and how many followers you had on each service. People would embed it on their sites and at the bottom there would be a link back to DuckDuckGo that said "new search engine."

This channel strategy worked beautifully. I was number one.

Trouble was, not a ton of people make that search—about fifty a day. So while I did get some traction and a steady stream of new users, it leveled off pretty quickly. It wasn't enough traction to be meaningful. It didn't move the needle.

I made two large traction mistakes here. First, I failed to have a concrete traction goal. In retrospect, to move the needle for my traction goals at the time, I needed more like five thousand new visitors a day, not fifty. Search engine optimization was not going to get me there.

Second, I was biased by my previous experience. Just because my last company got traction in this way didn't mean it was right for every company.

These are very natural mistakes to make. In fact, most startups make them. The most common startup trajectory now goes something like the following:

Founders have an idea for a company they're excited about. Initial excitement turns into a struggle to build a product, but they do get something out the door.

Launch!

The founders expected customers to beat a path to their door, but unfortunately that isn't happening. Getting traction was an afterthought, but now they are focused on it. They try what they know or what they've heard others do: some Facebook ads, a little local PR, and maybe a smattering of blog posts.

Then they run out of money and the company dies.

Sadly, this is the norm. Even sadder, often these products are actually on to something. That is, with the right traction strategy they might have actually been able to get traction and not go out of business.

Given my previous startup success I thought I knew what I was doing. I was wrong. Luckily, I wasn't dead wrong. I had the money to self-fund through my traction mistakes, and so they didn't prove fatal for DuckDuckGo. Not everyone is as lucky.

Right when I realized I was making these mistakes I also realized I didn't know the right way to go about getting traction at all. I asked around. It turns out there was no good framework for getting traction, and that's how this book was born, way back in 2009.

Around this time I also started angel investing and more seriously advising other startups. I saw firsthand similar struggles and mistakes. I also partnered with Justin Mares, my coauthor. Justin founded two startups (one of which was acquired) and recently ran growth at Exceptional Cloud Services, which was acquired by Rackspace in 2013 for millions. He's a growth expert in his own right.

We set out to help startups get traction no matter what business they were in: from Internet companies to local small businesses and everything in between. We drew on our personal experiences, interviewed more than forty founders, studied many more companies, and pulled out the repeatable framework they used to succeed.

That framework is Bullseye, a simple three-step process for getting traction. Bullseye works for startups of all kinds: consumer or enterprise focused, large or small.

Since DuckDuckGo's humble beginnings, we have grown five orders of magnitude (10x growth spurts), from that initial one hundred searches a day to now over ten million a day. Each step—from 100 to 1,000, 10,000 to 100,000, 1,000,000 to 10,000,000—involved figuring out how to get traction again. That's because, as you will see, often what works in one growth stage eventually stops working.

Thankfully we had Bullseye to help us find the right traction channel strategy at the right time. After my search engine optimization mistake, we shifted to using content marketing, social and display ads, publicity, and most recently business development. We've hit the bull's-eye repeatedly, and so can you.

TRACTION

CHAPTER ONE

Traction Channels

Before we get started, let's define traction. Traction is a sign that your company is taking off. It's obvious in your core metrics: If you have a mobile app, your download rate is growing rapidly. If you're running a subscription service, your monthly revenue is skyrocketing. If you're an organic bakery, your number of transactions is increasing every week. You get the point.

Naval Ravikant, founder of AngelList, an online platform that helps companies raise money, says it well:

> Traction is basically quantitative evidence of customer demand. So if you're in enterprise software, [initial traction] may be two or three early customers who are paying a bit; if you're in consumer software the bar might be as high as hundreds of thousands of users.

You can always get more traction. The whole point of a startup is to grow rapidly. Getting traction means moving your growth curve up and to the right as best you can. Paul Graham, founder of startup accelerator Y Combinator, puts it like this:

> *A startup is a company designed to grow fast. Being newly founded does not in itself make a company a startup. Nor is it necessary for a startup to work on technology, or take venture funding, or have some sort of "exit." The only essential thing is growth. Everything else we associate with startups follows from growth.*

Traction is growth. The pursuit of traction is what defines a startup.

After interviewing more than forty successful founders and researching countless more, we discovered that startups get traction through *nineteen different channels.* Many successful startups experimented with multiple channels until they found one that worked.

We call these customer acquisition channels *traction channels.* These are marketing and distribution channels through which your startup can get traction: real customer growth.

We uncovered two broad themes through our research. First, most founders consider using only traction channels with which they're already familiar, or those they think they should be using because of their type of product or company. This means that far too many startups focus on the same channels and ignore other promising ways to get traction. In fact, often the most underutilized channels in an industry are the most promising ones.

Second, it's hard to predict the traction channel that will work best. You can make educated guesses, but until you start running tests, it's difficult to tell which channel is the best one for you right now.

Our introductory chapters 2–5 expand on these themes. Chapter 2 introduces you to traction thinking: the mind-set you need to adopt to maximize your chances of getting traction. Chapter 3 presents our framework for getting traction called Bullseye. Essentially, it involves targeted experimentation with a few traction channels, followed by laser focus on the core channel that is most promising.

Chapter 4 explains how to go about running traction tests, a central theme of Bullseye. Chapter 5 presents a second framework—called Critical Path—to help you focus on the right traction goal and ignore everything else not required to achieve it.

Before you jump into this material, however, we'd like to introduce you to the nineteen traction channels and some of the people we interviewed for them. We will explore each of these channels in chapters 6–24.

When going through the traction channels, try your best not to dismiss them as irrelevant for your company. Each traction channel has worked for startups of all kinds and phases. As mentioned, the right channel is often an underutilized one. Get one channel working that your competitors dismiss, and you can grow rapidly while they languish.

Targeting Blogs

Popular startups like Codecademy, Mint, and reddit all got their start by targeting blogs. Noah Kagan, Mint's former director of marketing, told us how he targeted niche blogs early on, and how this strategy allowed Mint to acquire forty thousand customers before launching.

Publicity

Publicity is the art of getting your name out there via traditional media outlets like newspapers, magazines, and TV. We interviewed Jason Kincaid, former *TechCrunch* writer, about pitching media outlets, how to form relationships with reporters, and what most startups do wrong when it comes to publicity. We also talked with Ryan Holiday, media strategist and bestselling author of *Trust Me, I'm Lying*, to learn how startups could leverage today's rapidly changing media landscape to get traction.

Unconventional PR

Unconventional PR involves doing something exceptional like publicity stunts to draw media attention. This channel can also work by repeatedly going above and beyond for your customers.

Alexis Ohanian told us some of the things he did to get people talking about reddit and Hipmunk, two startups he cofounded.

Search Engine Marketing

Search engine marketing (SEM) allows companies to advertise to consumers searching on Google and other search engines. We interviewed Matthew Monahan of Inflection, the company behind Archives.com (before its $100 million acquisition by Ancestry.com), to learn how Archives relied primarily on SEM for its growth.

Social and Display Ads

Ads on popular sites like reddit, YouTube, Facebook, Twitter, and hundreds of other niche sites can be a powerful and scalable way to reach new customers. We brought in Nikhil Sethi, founder of the social ad buying platform Adaptly, to talk with us about getting traction with social and display ads.

Offline Ads

Offline ads include TV spots, radio commercials, billboards, infomercials, newspaper and magazine ads, as well as flyers and other local advertisements. These ads reach demographics that are harder to target online, like seniors, less tech-savvy consumers, and commuters. Few startups use this channel, which means there's less competition for many of these audiences. We talked with Jason Cohen, founder of WP Engine and Smart Bear Software, about the offline ads he's used to acquire customers.

Search Engine Optimization

Search engine optimization (SEO) is the process of making sure your Web site shows up for key search results. We interviewed Rand Fishkin of Moz (the market leader in SEO software) to talk about best practices for getting traction with SEO. Patrick McKenzie, founder of Appointment Reminder, also explained to us how he uses SEO to cheaply acquire lots of highly targeted traffic.

Content Marketing
Many startups have blogs. However, most don't use their blogs to get traction. We talked with Unbounce founder Rick Perreault and OkCupid cofounder Sam Yagan to learn how their blogs transformed their businesses.

Email Marketing
Email marketing is one of the best ways to convert prospects while retaining and monetizing existing customers. For this chapter we interviewed Colin Nederkoorn, founder of email marketing startup Customer.io, to discuss how startups can get the most out of this traction channel.

Engineering as Marketing
Using engineering resources to acquire customers is a significantly underutilized way to get traction. Successful companies have built microsites, developed widgets, and created free tools that drive thousands of leads each month. We asked Dharmesh Shah, founder of HubSpot, to discuss how engineering as marketing has driven HubSpot's growth to tens of thousands of customers through tools like its Marketing Grader.

Viral Marketing
Viral marketing consists of growing your customer base by encouraging your customers to refer other customers. We interviewed Andrew Chen, a viral marketing expert and mentor at 500 Startups, for common viral techniques and the factors that have led to viral adoption in major startups. We also talked with Ashish Kundra of myZamana, who discussed using viral marketing to grow from 100,000 users to more than 4 million in less than a year.

Business Development
Business development (BD) is the process of creating strategic relationships that benefit both your startup and your partner. Paul

English, cofounder and CEO of Kayak.com, walked us through the impact of Kayak's early partnership with AOL. We also interviewed venture capitalist Chris Fralic, whose BD efforts at Half.com were a major factor in eBay's $350 million acquisition of the company. We'll show you how to structure deals, find strategic partners, build a business development pipeline, and approach potential partners.

Sales
Sales is focused primarily on creating processes to directly exchange product for dollars. We interviewed David Skok of Matrix Partners—someone who's taken four different companies public—to get his perspective on how the best software companies are creating sustainable, scalable sales processes. We also take a look at how to find early customers and have winning sales conversations.

Affiliate Programs
Companies like HostGator, GoDaddy, and Sprout Social have robust affiliate programs that have allowed them to reach hundreds of thousands of customers in a cost-effective way. We interviewed Kristopher Jones, founder of the Pepperjam affiliate network, to learn how a startup can leverage this channel. We also talked with Maneesh Sethi to learn how affiliate marketers choose which products to promote, and some of the strategies they use to do so.

Existing Platforms
Focusing on existing platforms means focusing your growth efforts on a megaplatform like Facebook, Twitter, or the App Store, and getting some of their hundreds of millions of users to use your product. Alex Pachikov, on the founding team of Evernote, explained how their focus on Apple's App Store generated millions of customers.

Trade Shows

Trade shows are a chance for companies in specific industries to show off their latest products. We interviewed Brian Riley of SureStop, an innovative bike brake startup, to learn how it sealed a partnership that led to more than twenty thousand sales from one trade show and its approach to getting traction at each event.

Offline Events

Sponsoring or running offline events—from small meetups to large conferences—can be a primary way to get traction. We spoke with Rob Walling, founder and organizer of MicroConf, to talk about how to run a fantastic event.

Speaking Engagements

Eric Ries, author of the bestselling book *The Lean Startup*, told us how he used speaking engagements to hit the bestseller list within a week of his book's launch. We also interviewed Dan Martell, founder of Clarity, to learn how to leverage a speaking event, give an awesome talk, and grow your startup's profile at such speaking gigs.

Community Building

Companies like Wikipedia and Stack Exchange have grown by forming passionate communities around their products. In our interview with Jeff Atwood of Stack Exchange, he detailed how he built the Stack Overflow community, which has created the largest repository of useful programming questions and answers in history.

After reading this book, you will appreciate how each of these nineteen traction channels could get traction for your business. You will be equipped with the framework to find out which one to focus on, and how to go about doing so.

CHAPTER TWO

Traction Thinking

How much time should you spend on getting traction? When should you start? How do you know if it's working? How much traction do you need to get investors? This chapter answers these and other general traction questions, empowering you with the traction thinking that will set you up for success.

THE 50 PERCENT RULE

If you're starting a company, chances are you can build a product. Almost every failed startup has a product. What failed startups don't have is enough customers.

Marc Andreessen, cofounder of Netscape and VC firm Andreessen Horowitz, sums up this common problem:

> *The number one reason that we pass on entrepreneurs we'd otherwise like to back is they're focusing on product to the*

exclusion of everything else. Many entrepreneurs who build great products simply don't have a good distribution strategy. Even worse is when they insist that they don't need one, or call [their] no distribution strategy a "viral marketing strategy."

A common story goes like this: Founders build something people want by spending their time making tweaks based on what early customers say they want. Then, when they think they are ready, they launch and take stabs at getting more customers, only to become frustrated when customers aren't flocking to them.

Having a product or service that your early customers love, but having no clear way to get more traction is a major problem. To solve this problem, spend your time constructing your product or service and testing traction channels *in parallel.*

Traction and product development are of equal importance and should each get about half of your attention. This is what we call the 50 percent rule: spend 50 percent of your time on product and 50 percent on traction.

Building something people want is certainly required for traction, but it isn't enough. There are four common situations where you could build something people want, but still not end up with a viable business.

First, you could build something people want, but for which you just can't figure out a viable business model. The money isn't adding up. For example, people won't pay, and selling advertising won't cover the bills. There is just no real market.

Second, you could build something people want, but there are just not enough customers to reach profitability. It's just too small a market, and there aren't obvious ways to expand. This occurs often when startups aren't ambitious enough and pick too narrow a niche.

Third, you could build something people want, but reaching them is cost prohibitive. You find yourself in a hard-to-reach market. An example is a relatively inexpensive product that requires a direct sales force to sell it. That combo just doesn't work.

Finally, you could build something people want, but a lot of other companies build it too. In this situation you are in a hypercompetitive market where it is simply too hard to get customers.

If you follow the 50 percent rule from the beginning, then you will have the best chance of avoiding these traps. If you don't, then you risk realizing you're in one of these traps too late to do anything useful. Unfortunately this happens to a lot of companies postlaunch. The sad thing is that often these products and services are useful, but the companies die because they don't have a good distribution strategy.

The flip side is that if you focus on traction from the beginning, then you can figure out very quickly if you're on the right track. The results from your traction experiments will guide you around these traps and toward the traction channel that will drive the most meaningful growth.

This 50 percent rule is hard to follow because the pull to spend all of your attention on product is strong. After all, you probably got into your startup because you wanted to build a particular product or service. You had a vision. A lot of the traction activities are unknown and outside of both your comfort zone and this initial vision. That's why there is a natural tendency to avoid them. Don't.

To be clear, splitting your time evenly between product and traction will certainly slow down product development. However, it counterintuitively won't slow the time to get your product successfully to market. In fact, it will speed it up! That's because pursuing product development and traction in parallel has a couple of key benefits.

First, it helps you build *the right* product because you can incorporate knowledge from your traction efforts. If you're following a good product development process, you're already getting good feedback from early customers. However, these customers are generally too close to you. They often tell you what you want to hear.

Through traction development you get a steady stream of cold customers. It is through these people that you can really find out whether the market is taking to your product or not, and if not, what features are missing or which parts of the experience are broken.

You can think of your initial investment in traction as pouring water into a leaky bucket. At first your bucket will be very leaky because your product is not yet a full solution to customer needs and problems. In other words, your product is not as sticky as it could be, and many customers will not want to engage with it yet. As a consequence, much of the money you are spending on traction will leak out of your bucket.

This is exactly where most founders go wrong. They think because this money is leaking out that it is money wasted. Oppositely, this process is telling you where the real leaks are in your bucket (product). If you don't interact with cold customers in this way, then you generally spend time on the wrong things in terms of product development.

These interactions also get you additional data, like what messaging is resonating with potential customers, what niche you might focus on first, what types of customers will be easiest to acquire, and what major distribution roadblocks you might run into.

You will get some of this information through good product development practices, but not nearly enough. All of this new information should change the first version of the product for the better and inform your distribution strategy.

This is exactly what happened with Dropbox. While developing their product, they tested search engine marketing and found it wouldn't work for their business. They were acquiring customers for $230 when their product cost only $99. That's when they focused on the viral marketing traction channel, and built a referral program right into their product. This program has since been their biggest growth driver.

In contrast, waiting until you launch a product to embark on traction development usually results in one or more additional product development cycles as you adjust to real market feedback. That's why doing traction and product development in parallel may slow down product development in the short run, but in the long run it's the opposite.

The second key benefit to parallel product and traction development is that you get to experiment and test different traction channels before you launch anything. This means when your product is ready, you can grow rapidly. A head start on understanding the traction channel that will work for your business is invaluable. Phil Fernandez, founder and

CEO of Marketo, a marketing automation company that IPO'd in 2013, talks about this benefit:

> *At Marketo, not only did we have SEO [search engine optimization] in place even before product development, we also had a blog. We talked about the problems we aimed to solve. . . . Instead of beta testing a product, we beta tested an idea and integrated the feedback we received from our readers early on in our product development process.*
>
> *By using this content strategy, we at Marketo began drumming up interest in our solutions with so much advance notice we had a pipeline of more than fourteen thousand interested buyers when the product came to market.*

Marketo wouldn't have had fourteen thousand interested buyers if they just focused on product development. It's the difference between significant customer growth on day one—real traction—and just a product you know some people want.

MOVING THE NEEDLE

Before you can set about getting traction, you have to define what traction means for your company. You need to set a traction goal. At the earliest stages, this traction goal is usually to get enough traction to either raise funding or become profitable. In any case, you should figure out what this goal means in terms of hard numbers. How many customers do you need and at what growth rate?

Your traction strategy should always be focused on moving the needle for your traction goal. By moving the needle, we mean focusing on marketing activities that result in a measurable, significant impact on your traction goal. It should be something that advances your user acquisition goal in a meaningful way, not something that would be just a blip even if it worked.

For example, early on DuckDuckGo focused on search engine optimization to get in front of users searching for "new search engine." This focus was successful at obtaining users, but did not bring in enough users to get close to the traction goal. It didn't move the needle.

From the perspective of getting traction, you can think about working on a product or service in three phases:

Phase I—making something people want
Phase II—marketing something people want
Phase III—scaling your business

In the leaky bucket metaphor, phase I is when your bucket (product) has the most leaks. It really doesn't hold water. There is no reason to scale up your efforts now, but it is still important to send a small amount of water through the bucket so you can see where the holes are and plug them.

When you constantly test traction channels by sending through a steady stream of new customers, you can tell if your product is getting less leaky over time, which it should be if your product development strategy is sound. In fact this is a great feedback loop between traction development and product development that you can use to make sure you're on the right track.

As you hone your product, you are effectively plugging leaks. Once you have crossed over to phase II, you have product-market fit and customers are sticking around. Now is the time to scale up your traction efforts: your bucket is no longer leaky. You are now fine-tuning your positioning and marketing messages.

In phase III, you have an established business model and significant position in the market, and are focused on scaling both to further dominate the market and to profit.

In each phase you will find yourself generally focused on different things because moving the needle means different things as you grow. In phase I, it's getting those first customers that prove your product can get traction. In phase II, it is getting enough customers that you're knocking on the door of sustainability. And in phase III, your focus is on increasing your earnings, scaling your marketing channels, and creating a truly sustainable business.

Phase I is very product focused and involves pursuing initial traction while also building your initial product. This often means getting traction in ways that don't scale—giving talks, writing guest posts, emailing people you have relationships with, attending conferences, and doing whatever you can to get in front of customers.

As Paul Graham said in his essay "Do Things That Don't Scale":

> *A lot of would-be founders believe that startups either take off or don't. You build something, make it available, and if you've made a better mousetrap, people beat a path to your door as promised. Or they don't, in which case the market must not exist.*
>
> *Actually startups take off because the founders make them take off. . . . The most common unscalable thing founders have to do at the start is to recruit users manually. Nearly all startups have to. You can't wait for users to come to you. You have to go out and get them.*

Startup growth happens in spurts. Initially, growth is usually slow. Then it spikes as a useful traction channel strategy is unlocked. Eventually it flattens out again as this strategy gets saturated and becomes less effective. Then you unlock another strategy and you get another spike.

As your company grows, smaller traction strategies stop moving the needle. If you have ten thousand visitors to your Web site each day, it will be hard to appreciate a tweet or blog post that sends twenty visitors your way.

Moving the needle in the later stages requires larger and larger numbers. If you want to add 100,000 new customers, with conversion rates between 1 and 5 percent, you're looking at reaching 2 to 10 million people in a targeted marketing campaign—those are huge numbers! That's why traction channels like community building and viral marketing can be so powerful: they scale with the size of your user base and potential market. In any case, always consider your traction efforts in terms of whether they are moving the needle for your traction goal.

HOW MUCH TRACTION IS ENOUGH FOR INVESTORS?

Startup founders hoping to scale quickly tend to focus on fund-raising. Not every company starts off planning on an eventual IPO, but any that do need outsiders buying in. As a result, they often wonder how much traction they need to get investors interested. Naval Ravikant, founder of AngelList, answered this question well a few years ago:

> It is a moving target. The entire ecosystem is getting far more efficient. Companies are accomplishing a lot more with a lot less.
>
> Two years ago [November 2010] you could have gotten your daily deal startup funded pre-traction. Eighteen months ago you could not have gotten a daily deal startup funded no matter how much traction you had. Twelve months ago you could have gotten your mobile app company funded with ten thousand downloads. Today it's probably going to take a few hundred thousand downloads and a strong rapid adoption rate for a real financing to take place.
>
> The definition of traction keeps changing as the environment gets competitive. That's why it is actually useful to look at AngelList and look at companies who just got funded; that will give you an idea of where the bar is right now.

When pursuing funding, first contact individuals who intimately understand what you're working on (perhaps because they have worked on or invested in something similar before).

The better your prospective investors understand what you're doing, the less traction they will need to see before they invest because they are more likely to extrapolate your little traction and believe it could grow into something big. On the other hand, those investors who have little real-world experience within your industry may find it hard to extrapolate and may demand more traction initially before they invest. An outlier is friends and family, who may not need to see any traction before investing, because they're investing in you personally.

It is easy to get discouraged when you are fund-raising because you can get so many rejections. However, you shouldn't take rejection as a rejection of your idea. There are many reasons why investors may say no that are simply beyond your control (investment goals, timing, expertise, etc.).

Sustainable product engagement growth (i.e., more customers getting engaged over time) is hard for any investor to ignore. This is true even if your absolute numbers are relatively small. So if you have only a hundred customers, but have been growing 10 percent a month for six months, that's attractive to investors. With sustainable growth, you look like a good bet to succeed in the long run. With investing, always remember that *traction trumps everything*.

TO PIVOT OR NOT TO PIVOT

You may come to a point where you are simply unhappy with your traction. You may not be able to raise funding or you may just feel like things aren't taking off the way they should. How do you know when to "pivot" from what you're doing?

We strongly believe that many startups give up way too early. A lot of startup success hinges on choosing a great market at the right time. Consider DuckDuckGo, the search engine startup that Gabriel founded. Other search startups gave up after two years: Gabriel has been at it for more than seven.

Privacy has been a core differentiator for DuckDuckGo (it does not track you) since 2009 but didn't become a mainstream issue until the NSA leaks in 2013. Growth was steady before 2013, but exploded when privacy became an item on the national consciousness.

It's important to wrap your head around this timescale. If you are just starting out, are you ready to potentially do this for the *next decade*? In retrospect, a lot of founders feel they picked their company idea too quickly, and they would have picked something they were more passionate about if they had realized it was such a long haul. A startup can be awesome if you believe in it: if not, it can get old quickly.

If you are considering a pivot, the first thing to look for is evidence of real product engagement, even if it is only a few dedicated customers. If you have such engagement, you might be giving up too soon. You should examine these bright spots to see how they might be expanded. Why do these customers take to your product so well? Is there some thread that unites them? Are they early adopters in a huge market or are they outliers? The answers to these questions may reveal some promise that is not immediately evident in your core metrics.

Another factor to consider before you pivot: startup founders are usually forward thinking and as a result are often too early to market, which is another reason why it's important to choose a startup idea you're willing to stick with for many years. Granted, there is a big difference between being a few years too early and a decade too early. Hardly anyone can stick around for ten years with middling results. But being a year or two early can be a great thing. You can use this time to improve and refine your product. Then, when the market takes off, you have a head start on competitors just entering your space.

How can you tell whether you are just a bit early to market and should keep plugging away? Again, the best way to find out is by looking for evidence of product engagement. If you are a little early to a market there should be some early adopters out there already eating up what you have to offer.

TARGETS

- **Put half your efforts into getting traction.** Pursue traction and product development in parallel, and spend equal time on both. Think of your product as a leaky bucket. Your early traction efforts are pointing you toward the holes worth plugging.

- **Set your growth goals.** Focus on strategies and tactics that can plausibly move the needle for your company. Get some hard numbers.
- **Learn what growth numbers potential investors respect.** How much traction is needed for investors is a moving target, but a sustainable customer growth rate is hard for investors to ignore. Potential investors who understand your business are likely to appreciate your traction and thus invest earlier. Traction trumps everything.
- **Find your bright spots.** If you're not seeing the traction you want, look for bright spots in your customer base, pockets of customers who are truly engaged with your product. See if you can figure out why it works for them and if you can expand from that base. If there are no bright spots, it may be a good time to pivot.

CHAPTER THREE
Bullseye

With nineteen traction channels to consider, figuring out which one to focus on is tough. That's why we've created a simple framework called Bullseye that will help you find *the channel* that will get you traction. As billionaire PayPal founder and early Facebook investor Peter Thiel put it:

> *[You] probably won't have a bunch of equally good distribution strategies. Engineers frequently fall victim to this because they do not understand distribution. Since they don't know what works, and haven't thought about it, they try some sales, BD, advertising, and viral marketing—everything but the kitchen sink.*
>
> *That is a really bad idea. It is very likely that one channel is optimal. Most businesses actually get zero distribution channels to work. Poor distribution—not product—is the number one cause of failure. If you can get even a single*

distribution channel to work, you have great business. If you try for several but don't nail one, you're finished. So it's worth thinking really hard about finding the single best distribution channel.

We use the name Bullseye for our three-step framework because you're aiming for the Bullseye—the one traction channel at the center of the target that will unlock your next growth stage.

THE OUTER RING: WHAT'S POSSIBLE

The first step in Bullseye is brainstorming every single traction channel. If you were to advertise offline, where would be the best place to do it? If you were to give a speech, who would be the ideal audience? Imagine what success would look like in each channel, and write it down in your outer ring.

Everyone starts off with biases. The outer ring is meant to help you systematically counteract your traction channel biases. It is important that you not dismiss any traction channel in this step. You should be able to think of at least one idea for every channel. In practice, a lot of founders mess up this step by not brainstorming long and deep enough to get useful ideas for each channel.

For each channel, you should identify one decent channel strategy that has a chance of moving the needle. For example, social ads is a traction channel. Specifically running ads on reddit, Twitter, or Facebook is a channel strategy within social ads. Through brainstorming, identify the best channel strategy you can think of in each of the nineteen traction channels.

In terms of research to feed your brainstorm, this book is a good start, but you should get much more specific to your company. You should know what marketing strategies have worked in your industry, as well as the history of companies in your space. It's especially important to understand how similar companies acquired customers over time, and how unsuccessful companies wasted their marketing dollars.

THE MIDDLE RING: WHAT'S PROBABLE

The second step in Bullseye is running cheap traction tests in the channels that seem most promising. Go around your outer ring and promote your best traction channel ideas to your middle ring.

It is often the case that there are a few truly exciting and promising channel ideas in your outer ring. Stop promoting ideas where there is an obvious drop-off in excitement. That drop-off often occurs around the third channel.

We want you to have more than one channel in your middle ring because we don't want you to waste valuable time testing channels sequentially when you can do so equally well in parallel. You can run multiple experiments at the same time because tests take some time to run after they've been set up. Yet doing too many things in parallel leads to errors from lack of focus, which means the number needs to be somewhat low.

For each traction channel in your middle ring, now construct a cheap traction test you can run to determine if the idea really is good or not. These tests should be designed to roughly answer the following three questions:

1. How much will it cost to acquire customers through this channel?
2. How many customers are available through this channel?
3. Are the customers that you are getting through this channel the kind of customers that you want right now?

There isn't a single method for testing each traction channel because every business is different. We will cover tactics for organizing and thinking about these tests in the next chapter. You should also get specific ideas for testing each traction channel throughout the rest of the book.

Some founders mess up this step by prematurely scaling their marketing efforts. Keep in mind that, when testing, you are not trying to get a lot of traction with a channel just yet. Instead, you are simply trying to determine if it's a channel that *could* move the needle for your startup. Your main consideration at this point is speed—to get data and to prove your assumptions.

You want to design smaller-scale tests that don't require much up-front cost or effort. For example, run four Facebook ads versus forty. You should be able to get a rough idea of a channel's effectiveness with at most a thousand dollars and a month of time. Often, it will be cheaper and shorter.

THE INNER RING: WHAT'S WORKING

The third and final step in Bullseye is to focus solely on the channel that will move the needle for your startup: your core channel.

If all went well, one of the traction channels you tested in your middle ring produced promising results. In that case, you should start directing all your traction efforts and resources toward this most promising channel. You hit the Bullseye! You've found your core channel.

At any stage in a startup's life cycle, one traction channel dominates in terms of customer acquisition. That is why we suggest focusing on one at a time, but only after you've identified a channel that seems like it could actually work.

The goal of this focusing step is quite simple: to wring every bit of traction out of your core channel. To do so, you will be continually experimenting to find out exactly how to optimize growth in this traction channel. As you dive deeper into it, you will uncover effective tactics and do everything you can to scale them until they are no longer effective due to saturation or rising costs.

The way this step gets most often messed up by founders is by keeping around distracting marketing efforts in other traction channels. For example, suppose you ran tests in three traction channels: search engine marketing, trade shows, and publicity. Search engine marketing was the most promising, and so you decide to focus on it and make it your core channel. However, your trade show and publicity tests were also successful, albeit much less so.

There is a natural tendency to do more trade shows and publicity because you know they will somewhat work. This is a mistake. Search engine marketing was significantly better, and so you should spend all your efforts on this core channel because uncovering additional strategies and tactics within it will have a greater effect than using these secondary channels. They're distracting.

This is additionally confusing because oftentimes focusing on your core channel involves channel strategies that utilize other traction channels. One channel is still dominant, but others feed into it.

For example, you will see that a focus on search engine optimization (SEO) requires getting links to your site, and a good tactic for getting links is getting publicity (another traction channel). Similarly, viral marketing is often built on email marketing or existing platforms like Facebook (two other traction channels). Yet in both these situations one channel is dominant in that it is your core traction strategy. You're using these other channels to support that strategy, as opposed to pursuing multiple traction strategies at once.

If, unfortunately, no channel seems promising after testing, the whole process should be repeated. The good news is you now have data from all the tests you just did, which will inform you as to what types of things are, and are not, resonating with customers. Look at the messaging you've been using, or dig deeper to see at what point each channel failed to deliver customers. If you go through the process several times and no traction channel seems promising, then your product may require more tweaking. Your bucket is still too leaky.

WHY USE BULLSEYE?

Bullseye is designed to be a straightforward way to direct your traction focus and maximize your results. First and foremost, it forces you to take all the traction channels more seriously than you would otherwise. These steps systematically uncover strategies for getting traction that you wouldn't have found using other approaches.

When we looked at companies really taking off, they were usually employing underutilized channels and channel strategies. If everyone in your industry uses social ads to grow, you might be better off using another channel. However, in this scenario social ads are probably what you know best because that is what everyone is using. Let Bullseye help you break out of your comfort zone and try channels that are unfamiliar because they may be the key to your growth.

Bullseye is also meant to help you zoom in on the best ideas as quickly and cheaply as possible, while still casting a wide net. The traction channel that will ultimately succeed is unpredictable, and time is of the essence. That's why we focus on successive rounds of quick parallel tests. It's simple and it works.

Noah Kagan talked to us about how he used a version of Bullseye at Mint, a site that helps you track your finances and was acquired by Intuit for $170 million. Its initial traction goal was 100,000 customers in the first six months after launch.

Noah and his team brainstormed and picked several traction channels that seemed promising (targeting blogs, publicity, search engine marketing). Then they ran a series of cheap tests in each (sponsored a small newsletter, contacted financial celebrities like Suze Orman, placed some Google ads) to see what worked and what didn't. Noah kept track of the test results in this spreadsheet:

SOURCE	TRAFFIC	CTR	CONVER-SION %	TOTAL USERS	STATUS	CONFIRMED	CONFIRMED USERS
Tech Crunch	300,000	10%	25%	7,500	Friend	Yes	7,500
Dave McClure	30,000	10%	25%	750	Friend	Yes	750
Mashable	500,000	10%	25%	12,500	Emailing	No	0
reddit	25,000	100%	25%	6,250	Coordinated	Yes	6,250
Digg	100,000	100%	25%	25,000	Coordinated	Yes	25,000
Google Organic	5000	100%	15%	750	Receiving	Yes	750
Google Ads	1,000,000	3%	35%	10,500	Bought	Yes	10,500
Paul Stamatiou	50,000	5%	50%	1,250	Friend	Yes	1,250
Personal Finance Sponsorships	200,000	40%	65%	52,000	Coordinated	Yes	52,000
Okdork.com	3,000	10%	75%	225	Self	Yes	225
Total Users				116,725			104,225

After running these experiments, Mint focused on the traction channel that seemed most promising and that could move the needle for its traction goal. In this case, that meant targeting blogs was its core channel. In the early days, the channel strategies of sponsoring mid-level bloggers in the financial niche and guest posting allowed Mint to acquire its first forty thousand customers.

When this channel maxed out and stopped moving the needle, Mint repeated the Bullseye process, and found a new core traction channel to focus on: publicity. Within six months of launching, it had 1 million users.

We heard stories like this over and over again when talking to successful startup founders. They would research many channels, try a few in parallel, and focus on the most promising until it stopped working. Bullseye is designed to systemize this successful process. Use it!

COMPARISON TO LEAN

Many good product development methodologies exist, but they don't deal explicitly with getting traction. The Lean Startup framework is a popular one. This approach involves creating testable hypotheses regarding your product, and then going out and validating (or invalidating) those hypotheses. It's an approach that demands a great deal of interaction with customers, discovering their needs and understanding the types of features they require.

Bullseye works hand in hand with Lean or with any other product development framework. What Lean is to product development, Bullseye is to traction.

The biggest mistake startups make when trying to get traction is failing to pursue traction in parallel with product development. Many entrepreneurs think that if you build a killer product, your customers will beat a path to your door. This line of thinking is a fallacy: that the best use of your time is always improving your product. In other words, "if you build it, they will come" is *wrong*.

You are much more likely to develop a good distribution strategy with a good traction development methodology (like Bullseye) the same way you are much more likely to develop a good product with a good product development methodology (like Lean). Both help address major risks that face early-stage companies: market risk (that you can reach customers in a sustainable way) and product risk (that customers want what you're building).

Pursuing both traction and product in parallel will increase your chances of success by both developing a product for which you can actually get traction and getting traction with that product much sooner.

TARGETS

- **Work through Bullseye.** Maximize your chances of getting traction: brainstorm, prioritize, test, and then focus. Do not overlook underutilized channels. In fact, those channels are more likely to be the ones that will work best.
- **Talk to founders a few steps ahead of you.** Research how past and present companies in your space and adjacent spaces succeeded or failed at getting traction. The easiest way to do this is to go talk to startup founders who previously failed at what you're trying to do.
- **Hold on to your other channel ideas.** Compile your brainstorming ideas for each traction channel in a spreadsheet with educated guesses that you can confirm through testing. Even after you've chosen your core channel, you should keep these ideas around for future runs of Bullseye.

CHAPTER FOUR

Traction Testing

Continuous testing is the key to getting traction with Bullseye. When searching for a traction channel to focus on, you're testing the channels in your middle ring to see which is the most promising. Then, when you find one worth your undivided attention, you test strategies and tactics within that core channel to wring the most traction from it. In this chapter, we cover how to approach testing.

MIDDLE RING TESTS

The goal of middle ring tests is to find a promising channel strategy to focus on. A channel strategy is a particular way to acquire customers within a channel. For example, offline ads is a traction channel, and billboards, transit ads, and magazine ads are all channel strategies within offline ads. When you're just starting out testing a channel, you will pick one channel strategy to pursue—the most promising one you came up with when brainstorming.

In particular, your tests should be designed to answer these questions:

1. How much does it cost to acquire each customer through this channel strategy?
2. How many customers are available through this channel strategy?
3. Are the customers you are getting through this channel the ones you want right now?

With limited resources, it's almost impossible to optimize multiple channel strategies at once. Running ten social ads and testing everything about them (ad copy, landing pages, etc.) is a full-time endeavor. That is *optimization*, not testing. Rather, you should be running several cheap tests (perhaps two social ads with two landing pages) that give some indication of how successful a given channel strategy could be. In other words, you should not be getting too deep into tactics at this stage; stick to the strategy level.

These first channel strategy tests are often very cheap and short. For instance, if you spend just $250 on AdWords, you'll get a rough idea of how well the search engine marketing channel works for your business. In general in phase I, you shouldn't be spending more than a thousand dollars and a month's time on a middle ring test, and often significantly less. When you're further along in phases II and III, channel tests may be bigger and longer because you need bigger numbers to move the needle for your traction goal.

Middle ring tests arm you with data that you can use to compare channel strategies. If all goes well, you hit the Bullseye and can move on to inner ring testing.

INNER RING TESTS

Inner ring tests are designed to do two things. First, to optimize your chosen channel strategy to make it the best it can be. Second, to uncover better channel strategies within this traction channel.

Really focusing on a traction channel takes significant time and resources. This time is valuable and should be used only after you have some indication that the chosen channel will likely work. You should have an idea it will likely work because this channel strategy emerged from middle ring testing.

In terms of optimization, each channel strategy has a set of things you can tweak. For example, for targeting blogs you can tweak which blogs to target, what type of content to push, and what the call to action is in this content. For search engine marketing, you can tweak keywords, ad copy, demographics, and landing pages.

You should be continually testing your chosen channel strategy in an effort to increase its effectiveness. These tests should be scientific so you have confidence you are tweaking things in the right direction. A common approach is to use some form of A/B testing (also known as split testing).

In its most basic form, A/B testing is a science experiment with a control group (A) and an experimental group (B). A/B testing is often called split testing because for the best results you split people randomly into one of the two groups, and then measure what they do.

The purpose of an A/B test is to measure the effectiveness of a change in one or more variables—a button color, an ad image, or a different message on one of your Web pages. You create one version of your page for your control group and a second version for your experimental group. As you track how each page performs, you can find out whether your changes are having an impact on a key metric like signups. If, after a period of time, the experimental group performs significantly better, you can apply the change, reap the benefits, and run another test.

Making A/B testing a habit (even if you run just one test a week) will improve your efficiency in a traction channel by two or three times. There are many tools to help you do this type of testing online, such as Optimizely, Visual Website Optimizer, and Unbounce. These tools allow you to test optimizations without making complex changes to your code.

In addition to optimization testing, you should also be testing additional channel strategies within your core channel. These resemble middle ring tests in that they should initially be cheap and fast and answer the same basic questions as middle ring tests. The goal here is to see if there is a better channel strategy you should be using within your core channel.

Once you truly focus on a channel, you will become an expert in it. Channel experts uncover new channel strategies and tactics, which are often the best ones simply because they are new. That should be your goal with additional channel strategy testing.

Andrew Chen, a startup adviser on growth, coined the Law of Shitty Click-Throughs: "Over time, all marketing strategies result in shitty click-through rates." ("Click-through rate" refers to the response rate of a marketing campaign.)

What this means is that over time, all marketing channels become saturated. As more companies discover an effective strategy, it becomes crowded and expensive or ignored by consumers, thus becoming much less effective. When banner ads first debuted, they were receiving click-through rates of over 75 percent! Once they became commonplace, click-through rates plummeted.

This happens with all channel strategies. Tactics that once worked well will become crowded and ineffective. All it takes is one other competitor seriously pursuing traction in the same way to drive up its cost and drive down its efficacy.

It is likely that your first channel strategy ideas are commonplace and have already succumbed somewhat to the Law of Shitty Click-Throughs. To combat this reality you should consistently brainstorm new channel strategies and conduct small experiments. Constantly running small traction tests will allow you to stay ahead of competitors pursuing the same channels. As Andrew puts it:

> The . . . solution to solving the Law of Shitty Click-Throughs, even momentarily, is to discover the next untapped marketing [strategy]. . . . If you can make these [strategies] work with a strong product behind [them], then great. Chances are,

you'll enjoy a few months if not a few years of strong market-
ing performance before they too slowly succumb.

An untapped channel strategy may mean trying something different in an established venue, but it also could mean trying a venue no one else is using. For example, you might be able to take advantage of new marketing platforms while they are still in their infancy.

Zynga (the maker of FarmVille and other games) did this with Facebook, dominating its advertising and sharing features when there was relatively little competition. For a gaming company today, it's basically impossible to leverage Facebook to grow the way Zynga did just a few years ago—it's just too expensive and too crowded. However, the company that leverages a newer platform that's growing quickly will have a significant advantage over companies chasing the same old methods.

Another place to look for underutilized channel strategies is in using other traction channels to feed into your core traction channel. As we discussed previously, you do not want to focus separately on multiple traction channels. However, you can utilize other channels as part of your core channel strategy.

For example, suppose your core channel is content marketing, centered around your company blog. To jump-start your blog you may target other blogs for guest posts (in the targeting blogs channel). You might also buy social ads to amplify your best posts on Twitter and Facebook (in the social and display ads channel). In both these cases, you are not solely focusing on these secondary channels to get growth; you are using them to feed into your content marketing strategy.

Now, both of those examples are pretty standard. What if you could find a way to use community building, speaking engagements, or offline ads to jump-start your content marketing strategy? Once you have a core traction channel, it is often instructive to brainstorm the other eighteen traction channels in terms of how you might use them to support your core channel. Doing so could uncover some truly novel channel strategies that haven't yet succumbed to the Law of Shitty Click-Throughs.

ONLINE TOOLS

As testing is central to getting traction, you should seek online tools to help you organize and execute your tests, even if they are offline tests. Sean Ellis, growth adviser to Dropbox and Eventbrite, had this to say about this approach:

> *The faster you run high-quality experiments, the more likely you'll find scalable, effective growth tactics. Determining the success of a customer acquisition idea is dependent on an effective tracking and reporting system, so don't start testing until your tracking/reporting system has been implemented.*

This "effective tracking and reporting system" can be as simple as a spreadsheet or as complex as an analytics tool that does cohort analysis, but it must exist. Furthermore, each test you run should have a point—to validate or invalidate specific assumptions you specify ahead of time.

Every day more online tools come on the market to help you optimize traction channels. We highly recommend embracing the use of online tools to help you understand and assess the efficacy of all your traction efforts.

For example, the questions below seem like they are difficult or might require a lot of research to answer:

- How many prospective customers landed on my Web site?
- What are the demographics of my best and worst customers?
- Are customers who interact with my support team more likely to stay customers longer?

However, they are quite straightforward if you're using the right online tools. In fact, a basic analytics tool like Clicky, Mixpanel, or Chartbeat can help you answer all three of these questions. These tools tell you who is coming to your site, at what frequency, and, perhaps most important, when and where they are leaving your site.

We recommend using a spreadsheet to help you rank and prioritize your traction channel strategies. The questions you are answering from tests all have numeric answers, and so a spreadsheet is a natural tool to use.

At a minimum, include the columns of *how many customers are available, conversion rate, cost to acquire a customer,* and *lifetime value of a customer* for a given strategy. Because these metrics are universal, you can use them to easily make comparisons across strategies. In general, we encourage you to be as quantitative as possible, even if it is just guesstimating at first.

As we mentioned earlier, you should be thinking about only those traction channels and specific strategies that have a chance of moving the needle for your traction goal. You can assess what can move the needle with some simple calculations. How many new customers do you need to really move the needle?

If there is no reasonable chance that a channel strategy could yield enough new customers to move the needle within your current budget, then it is not worth exploring further. For example, focusing on getting articles on tech news sites doesn't make sense right now for DuckDuckGo because they couldn't possibly convert enough people to make a significant difference in the company's search numbers. However, this strategy did work in phase I.

Most channels will yield you some customers, and so they are all tempting to some degree. The operative question then is, "Does this channel have enough customers to be meaningful?" A simple spreadsheet calculation can go a long way!

TARGETS

- **Look for customers where others aren't looking.** Keep a lookout for the cutting-edge tactics that haven't yet succumbed to the Law of Shitty Click-Throughs. Run cheap tests to quickly validate assumptions and test new ideas.
- **Constantly optimize.** You should consistently run A/B tests in your efforts to optimize a traction channel strategy. There are many online tools that can help you test more

easily and evaluate your use of various traction strategies and tactics.

- **Keep it numerical.** Look for ways to quantify your marketing efforts, especially when deciding which traction strategies to pursue and comparing them within Bullseye. You should have an idea at all times of what numbers it will take to move the needle, and focus your traction efforts only on strategies that could possibly do so.

CHAPTER FIVE
Critical Path

Startups get pulled in a lot of different directions. There are always opportunities in front of you or on the horizon that you could focus on. There are always product or service revisions you could work on. There are always background tasks nagging at you. How do you decide what to work on?

DEFINING YOUR TRACTION GOAL

You should always have an explicit traction goal you're working toward. This could be one thousand paying customers, one hundred new daily customers, or 10 percent of your market.

As we say, *traction trumps everything*. Because of that, what you choose to focus on should relate directly back to your traction goal.

The right goal is highly dependent on your business. It should be chosen carefully and align with your company strategy. You want a goal where hitting the mark would change things significantly for your company's outcome. Perhaps you'd be profitable, be able to raise money more easily, or become the market leader.

At DuckDuckGo the current traction goal is 1 percent of the general search market. Achieving that goal is meaningful because at that point the company will be taken much more seriously as an entrenched part of the market and everything that comes with that recognition (better deals, publicity, etc.).

This traction goal wouldn't work well for most other companies because usually 1 percent of a well-defined market is not that significant or valuable. It works in the general search engine space because the market is so big and there are so few companies in it. This speaks to the importance of setting a traction goal that is particularly significant for your company.

Before this traction goal, DuckDuckGo had a traction goal of 100 million searches a month, which took it to about a break-even point. Getting to breakeven was the company significance for that traction goal.

Before that the goal was to get the product and messaging to a point where people were switching to DuckDuckGo as their primary search engine. The company significance there was to move from phase I to II and get true product/market fit.

The importance of choosing the right traction goal cannot be overstated. Are you going for growth or profitability, or something in between? If you need to raise money in X months, what traction do you need to show to do so? These are the types of questions that help you determine the right traction goal.

Once that is defined, you can work backward and set clear quantitative and time-based traction subgoals, such as reaching one thousand customers by next quarter or hitting 20 percent monthly growth targets. Clear subgoals provide accountability. By placing traction activities on the same calendar as product development and other company milestones, you ensure that enough of your time will be spent on traction. We hope it is at least half of your time!

DEFINING YOUR CRITICAL PATH

The path to reaching your traction goal with the fewest number of steps is your Critical Path. You should literally enumerate the intermediate steps (milestones) to get to your traction goal. These milestones need not be traction related, but they should be *absolutely necessary* to reach your goal.

In DuckDuckGo's case, the traction goal was to get to 100 million searches a month. The team believed the milestones they needed to hit included a faster site, a more compelling mobile offering, and more broadcast TV coverage (from the publicity traction channel).

Even though product features like images and auto-suggest were continually requested, they believed they were not absolutely necessary milestones in their Critical Path to reach that traction goal. However, now that they are on the traction goal to get to 1 percent of the search market, these product features are believed to be necessary milestones on this new Critical Path.

The reasoning for why these particular features weren't necessary initially was that even at 100 million searches a month, DuckDuckGo's user base was motivated enough by other features to be forgiving of missing these particular ones. However, to get to the next traction goal the company had to get more mainstream adoption, and this next set of users is much less forgiving.

In your company, your milestones will be different, but the point is to be critical and strategic in deciding what to include. That's why it is called the *Critical* Path. For example, you may think that to reach your traction goal you will need to hire three people, add features A, B, and C to your product, and engage in marketing activities X, Y, and Z. These are the *milestones* you need to do to get where you want to go.

Do you really need feature C or marketing activity Y? This is where founders often mess up: by focusing their limited company resources on things off Critical Path. You are generally competing with companies with significantly more resources than you. You cannot afford to waste what little resources you have.

Another issue is that your original enumeration of necessary milestones is often wrong. For example, you thought you had to build features A, B, and C to get to your traction goal, but after building A and getting market feedback on it, you realize you actually need to skip B altogether and just build C. That's why a hard reassessment after each milestone is necessary. The best way to make sure you're not squandering your resources is to keep reevaluating whether what you're doing is on your Critical Path.

In other words, Critical Path is a framework to help you decide what *not* to do. Everything you decide to do should be assessed against your Critical Path. Every activity is either on path or not. If it is not on the path, don't do it!

OVERCOMING YOUR TRACTION BIASES

Bullseye is designed to help you find the best traction channel strategy to focus on as quickly as possible. Many founders unfortunately fail at applying Bullseye by ignoring promising traction channels due to natural biases. This is an expensive proposition as it wastes resources by sending you down the wrong path.

To refresh your memory, here are the nineteen channels:

1. Targeting Blogs
2. Publicity
3. Unconventional PR
4. Search Engine Marketing (SEM)
5. Social and Display Ads
6. Offline Ads
7. Search Engine Optimization (SEO)
8. Content Marketing
9. Email Marketing
10. Viral Marketing
11. Engineering as Marketing
12. Business Development (BD)
13. Sales

14. Affiliate Programs
15. Existing Platforms
16. Trade Shows
17. Offline Events
18. Speaking Engagements
19. Community Building

We're sure that some of these channels are unfamiliar to you. Why spend time and money on a channel you know little about, or that you think is irrelevant to your business?

Traction channel bias may be preventing you from getting traction. You can get a competitive advantage by acquiring customers in ways your competition isn't.

A major function of this book is simply helping you overcome your biases against particular traction channels by educating you about them. There are three reasons why founders ignore potentially profitable traction channels:

1. Out of sight, out of mind. Startups generally don't think of things like speaking engagements because they are usually out of their field of vision.
2. Some founders refuse to seriously consider channels they view negatively, like sales or affiliate marketing. Just because you hate talking on the phone doesn't mean your customers do.
3. Bias against schlep—things that seem annoying and time-consuming. Channels like business development and trade shows often fall into this category.

Be honest with yourself: which traction channels are you currently biased for or against? You can overcome these traction channel biases and increase your chances of success by taking each channel seriously when using Bullseye. Good mentors can also help you here by helping you brainstorm and rank your channel ideas. Jason Cohen, whom we interviewed for offline ads, makes this point well:

I'll bet you a lot of your competition will refuse to even try these channels. And if that's true, that's even more reason to go try those channels! It can almost be a competitive advantage (at least a temporary one) if you can acquire customers in channels that others cannot, or refuse to try. That's more interesting than duking it out with AdWords competitors in positions one to three.

Traction is a tricky thing. Initial traction is unpredictable and can happen in many different ways—nineteen by our count. Because of this unpredictability, it makes sense to consider several channels in the pursuit of traction. In fact, every one of the channels listed above has been *the* channel for both enterprise and consumer startups to get initial traction.

At the same time, no one individual is an expert on all channels. However, certain people—namely startup founders who focus on them—end up becoming experts on particular channels. We set out to collect and synthesize all this knowledge from founders and other experts with deep experience in each traction channel.

The startup experts we interviewed have founded companies that have made hundreds of millions of dollars, received billion-dollar valuations, and built some of the biggest companies. With this book, we're giving you what worked for these founders and arming you with the frameworks, strategies, and tactics to help you get similar traction.

We've already covered a system to figure out which channel to focus on—Bullseye—and how to go about doing so—Critical Path. The rest of the book helps you approach getting traction through each channel.

To your startup's success!

TARGETS

- **Lay out your milestones.** Determine your traction goal and define your Critical Path against that goal, working backward and enumerating the absolutely necessary milestones you need to achieve to get there.

- **Stay on the Critical Path.** Assess every activity you do against your Critical Path and consistently reassess it. Building such assessment into your management processes is a good idea. Quantify traction subgoals and put them on a calendar so you can properly monitor your progress over time.
- **Actively work to overcome your traction channel biases.** Being on the cutting edge of the right traction channel can make a huge difference in success. Which traction channels do you know most about? Which traction channels do you know least about? Mentors can help here.

CHAPTER SIX
Targeting Blogs

Targeting blogs prospective customers read is one of the most effective ways to get your first wave of customers. However, this traction channel can be difficult to scale in phases II and III due to the limited number of relevant high-traffic blogs. That's okay. Not all traction channels are infinitely scalable. In fact, using tactics that don't scale is one of the best ways to get your first customers. Paul Graham put it like this:

> *The need to do something unscalably laborious to get started is so nearly universal that it might be a good idea to stop thinking of startup ideas as scalars. Instead we should try thinking of them as pairs of what you're going to build, plus the unscalable thing(s) you're going to do initially to get the company going.*

We interviewed Noah Kagan, former head of marketing at Mint and founder of AppSumo, to learn how he used this channel to get significant initial traction for both startups by targeting blogs.

Mint's story is impressive. It launched its simple money management site in 2007, and—less than two years later—Intuit acquired it for $170 million. In between, Mint was able to acquire more than 1.5 million customers, 20,000 of whom signed up *before* it even launched. Within six months of Mint's launch, it had more than 1 million active users.

Very few startups experience this kind of growth during their first six months. Kagan, Mint's director of marketing at the time, drove many of its early marketing efforts. As he told us in our interview, Mint's phase I goal was to get 100,000 users within six months. To hit those numbers, Noah created a quant-based marketing spreadsheet like this:

SOURCE	TRAFFIC	CTR	CONVER-SION %	TOTAL USERS	STATUS	CONFIRMED	CONFIRMED USERS
Tech Crunch	300,000	10%	25%	7,500	Friend	Yes	7,500
Dave McClure	30,000	10%	25%	750	Friend	Yes	750
Mashable	500,000	10%	25%	12,500	Emailing	No	0
reddit	25,000	100%	25%	6,250	Coordinated	Yes	6,250
Digg	100,000	100%	25%	25,000	Coordinated	Yes	25,000
Google Organic	5000	100%	15%	750	Receiving	Yes	750
Google Ads	1,000,000	3%	35%	10,500	Bought	Yes	10,500
Paul Stamatiou	50,000	5%	50%	1,250	Friend	Yes	1,250
Personal Finance Sponsorships	200,000	40%	65%	52,000	Coordinated	Yes	52,000
Okdork.com	3,000	10%	75%	225	Self	Yes	225
Total Users				116,725			104,225

His spreadsheet listed traction channel strategies Mint planned to mine for potential customers. Then, Noah ran the numbers in terms of traffic, click-through rates (CTR), and conversions (actually signing up for the product in this case), and then calculated the number of expected customers from each channel strategy.

Next, he tested the channel strategies Mint might focus on by running tests on the ones that seemed promising. To test targeting blogs, he contacted a few that were representative of different customer segments and got them to write articles about Mint.

This should all sound pretty familiar at this point. Noah's method is an implementation of Bullseye: he systematically set out to determine which channel would allow him to accomplish his specific traction goal.

Mint's initial series of tests revealed that targeting blogs should be its core traction channel. Noah then created a long list of blogs to target, and set about focusing on this channel. Initially the focus was on more standard articles and guest posts. Through inner ring testing, Noah additionally uncovered channel strategies that further improved Mint's traction: VIP access and direct sponsoring.

Mint did something that few startups had done before to increase awareness and build excitement for its launch: it asked people on its prelaunch waiting list to recommend Mint to their friends in return for priority product access. As part of the signup process, users could embed an "I Want Mint" badge on their personal blogs, Facebook, or other Web sites. Users who drove signups through these badges were rewarded with VIP access before other invitations were sent out.

The key to the success of these badges was to make them easy to share and embed. Much as YouTube provides an embed code below each video on its site, Mint provided the code necessary to make embedding badges as simple as copying and pasting. Many users were happy to place the small badge on their Web site in order to get early access to a product they wanted. Mint had six hundred blogs display the badge and fifty thousand users signed up through them. This strategy also gave Mint an SEO boost from the hundreds of new links pointing to Mint.com.

Mint used a second innovative strategy to acquire customers through this traction channel: direct sponsoring of blogs. Each sponsored blog would place a small Mint advertisement on its site for a period of time. Noah tracked each advertisement to see which blogs were most effective and how many people signed up. Not only did this approach contribute more than ten thousand preregistrations for its product, but it also allowed the Mint team to understand the kind of customer most interested in its product.

Many personal bloggers have strong readerships, but don't make money from their writing. Noah offered them a way to show off a cool new service and make some money doing it. He simply sent them a message with "Can I send you $500?" as the subject and told them a bit about the product and what Mint was trying to do. Most were happy to share a useful product with their audiences and make some money in the process.

Mint also created content partnerships with larger sites like *The Motley Fool*, a personal investing site. With this content partnership (each site contributed content to the other), Mint exposed its valuable, free product to more than 3 million readers who would likely be interested in its service. This postlaunch content partnership combined targeting blogs with elements of business development and was a big win for the Mint team.

Noah used this traction channel again at AppSumo, his startup that sells software bundles and educational products at discounted prices. To get traction, Noah pulled together free bundles for blogs and conferences, such as SXSW.

One of the first bundles AppSumo did was specifically for *Lifehacker*, a popular productivity blog. Rather than just trying to pitch *Lifehacker* on his new startup, Noah built a product bundle for them before reaching out. *Lifehacker* couldn't turn down a bundle geared specifically toward its readers. In the blog's words:

> *Our love of free software here at Lifehacker is no secret, but sometimes you just need to shell out for some advanced features. AppSumo is currently offering a bundle of our favorite productivity webapps, for a fraction of the price.*

The offer did really well with *Lifehacker*'s audience, and led to strong early traction for AppSumo. Noah also sponsored blogs to run AppSumo giveaways, much as he did at Mint. AppSumo is now a profitable business with more than 800,000 customers.

TARGETING BLOG TACTICS

It can be difficult to uncover the smaller blogs that cover your niche. Here are several tools you can use to find all the influential bloggers in your space:

Search Engines—Simply search for things like "top blogs for x" or "best x blogs."

YouTube—Doing a simple search for your product keywords on YouTube shows you the most popular videos in your industry. These videos are often associated with influencers who have blogs, and you can use references to their videos as icebreakers to start building relationships with them. This tactic can be applied to other video sharing sites, such as Vimeo and Dailymotion.

Delicious—Delicious allows you to use keywords to find links that others have saved, which can unearth new blogs.

Twitter—Using Twitter search is another easy way to find blogs in a niche. You can also use tools like Followerwonk and Klout to determine the top Twitter accounts in your industry.

Social Mention—Social Mention helps you determine the sites that have the most frequent mentions for your keywords.

Talk to People—The most effective way to figure out what your target audience is really reading online is by asking them directly!

In addition to targeting blogs directly, you can also target the link-sharing communities that often link to them. Sharing links is at the heart of many large communities on the Web (e.g., reddit, Product Hunt, *Hacker News*, Inbound.org). In addition, there are hundreds of niche communities and forums that encourage and reward the sharing of links.

Dropbox, the file storage startup, targeted these communities for their initial traction. By sharing a video on *Hacker News*, Dropbox received more than ten thousand signups. Soon, it was trending on Digg (significantly bigger at the time), which drove even more signups.

Quora, Codecademy, and Gumroad saw similar success from initial postings on *Hacker News* because their products were a good fit for users of that site. The founders behind Filepicker.io—a file management tool for developers—also posted a basic demo there, looking for some feedback and early customers. Their submission was in the top spot for nearly three hours, during which they saw:

- 10,000+ visits
- 460 concurrent users
- 500+ developer signups
- 5,000+ files managed

In a crowded online environment, reaching prospects in an arena where they choose to spend their time is a valuable way to get traction. Targeting blogs and link-sharing communities can be a great way to get your first wave of customers.

TARGETS

- **Run tests on a variety of smaller blogs.** See what type of audience resonates best with your product and messaging. There are a variety of tools you can use to uncover relevant blogs, including YouTube, Delicious, StumbleUpon, Twitter, search engines, Google Alerts, and Social Mention. You can also ask people!
- **Sponsor small blogs, especially personal blogs.** Providing influential bloggers early access or offering early access in exchange for spreading the word are other effective strategies.
- **Offer something unique to your best targets.** Build a special offer just for them and put together a draft guest post that they can run with.

CHAPTER SEVEN
Publicity

Public relations (PR) traditionally refers to a company's public messaging of all kinds. In this chapter we focus on publicity from traditional media like news outlets, newspapers, and magazines.

Unconventional PR (like stunts and contests), content marketing, and targeting blogs are all related to publicity and can be magnified via this channel, but are covered individually in other chapters.

Starting out, an article in *TechCrunch* or a feature in *The Huffington Post* can boost your stature in the eyes of potential customers, investors, or partners. These mentions lead to larger features in news outlets like *The Washington Post* or *The New York Times*, which can move the needle for you in a matter of days. Publicity also has secondary benefits like helping with fund-raising, recruiting, and partnerships.

PUBLICITY STRATEGY

Startup founders are often unsure about how to get press. The first step is to understand how Internet-driven media works. Ryan Holiday, former director of marketing at American Apparel and bestselling author of *Trust Me, I'm Lying*, gave us a quick introduction:

> *The news has fundamentally changed. Think of* The New York Times. *When they decide to publish an article about you, they are doing you a huge favor. After all, there are so many other people they could write about.*
>
> *There are a finite number of spots in the paper. Blogs are different, as they can publish an infinite number of articles and every article they publish is a chance for more traffic (which means more money in their pockets). In other words, when* Business Insider *writes about you, you are doing them the favor.*

Most sites make their money from advertisements, so they want to drive as many page views as possible. If you have a fascinating story with broad appeal, media outlets now *want* to hear from you because you will drive visits and make them more money. This is why sites like *The Huffington Post* now churn out hundreds of articles a day: more articles drive more page views, which in turn allows them to make more money from advertisers.

There has also been a shift in how the top media outlets operate (CNN, *The New York Times*, the *Today* show). These organizations now scour smaller outlets for captivating stories they can present to a wider audience. As Ryan says:

> *It's better to start smaller when targeting big media outlets. For them, the direct approach is rarely the best approach. Instead, you approach obliquely. So you find the blogs that* TechCrunch *reads and gets story ideas from. Chances are it will be easier to get that blog's attention. You pitch there, which leads* The New York Times *to email you or do a story about you based on the information [they've seen] on their news radar.*

This means you no longer have to pitch CNN directly if you want to get on TV. Instead, you can pitch smaller sites (ones that are easier to get coverage from) whose content is often picked up by larger media outlets. If you tell your story right, you can create buzz around your company and capture the attention of larger sources. Next thing you know, you can put "As seen on CNN" on your Web site.

In other words, stories and other content now filter *up* the media chain, rather than *down*. Ryan again:

> *Blogs have an enormous influence over other blogs, making it possible to turn a post on a site with only a little traffic into posts on much bigger sites, if the latter happens to read the former. Blogs compete to get stories first, newspapers compete to "confirm" it, and then pundits compete for airtime to opine on it. The smaller sites legitimize the newsworthiness of the story for the sites with bigger audiences.*

Tech startups frequently get exposure this way. Sites like *TechCrunch* and *Lifehacker* often pick up stories from smaller forums like *Hacker News* and subreddits. In turn, *The New York Times* often picks up content from *TechCrunch* and wraps it into a larger narrative they're telling.

The story of DonorsChoose.org is an example of the modern-day media chain in action. DonorsChoose is a site that allows teachers to raise money for classroom projects, such as buying a digital microscope for a science class.

Many teachers in New York City were using the site to raise money, and several local outlets reported about this effort. Soon after, *Newsweek* picked it up. The *Newsweek* story received some attention, but nothing major. Then Oprah happened.

One of Oprah's people saw the article in *Newsweek* and she decided to name DonorsChoose as one of Oprah's favorite things for 2010. This national attention from Oprah led to sponsorship from the Gates Foundation and a major increase in donations.

Though media outlets are increasingly on the lookout for good stories, there are still challenges to getting exposure. Tens of thousands of companies are clamoring for media coverage. Jason Kincaid, a former reporter at *TechCrunch*, told us that he personally got pitched more than fifty times every day.

What gets a reporter's attention? Milestones: raising money, launching a new product, breaking a usage barrier, a PR stunt, a big partnership, or a special industry report. Each of these events is interesting and noteworthy enough to potentially generate some coverage.

Jason advises bundling smaller announcements together into one big announcement whenever possible. Breaking a usage barrier is great. Releasing a new version is noteworthy. But releasing a new version *and* breaking a usage barrier in the process is even more attractive to the press.

Below is an email pitch Jason Baptiste sent to *TechCrunch* just before launching PadPressed, his startup that helps blogs look better on iPads. It's a solid example of a good pitch: short, to the point, contains clear contact information, and links to a product demo. He even mentions he's happy to do a product giveaway, which makes this pitch even more enticing.

Subject: *Exclusive for TC: Launching PadPressed—make any blog feel like a native iPad app*

Hey Mike,

Launching PadPressed tomorrow at noon EST and TC gets free rein on an exclusive before then. PadPressed makes any blog look and behave like a native iPad app. We're talking accelerometer aware column resizing, swipe to advance articles, touch navigation, home screen icon support, and more. We've built some pretty cool tech to make this happen smoothly, and it works with your existing layout (iPad layout only activated when the blog is accessed from an iPad). Okay, I'll shut up now and you can check out the demo links/feature pages below, which are much more interesting than my pitch.

PS—Would also be happy to do giveaways to TC readers. Thanks again and feel free to reach out if you have any more questions (Skype, phone, etc. listed below).

Video Demo: http://vimeo.com/13487300
Live demo site (if you're on an iPad): jasonlbaptiste.com
Feature overviews: http://padpressed.com/features

Jason Kincaid warned against having your pitch come across as a "wall of text," something busy reporters who receive hundreds of emails get tired of seeing. Be succinct and clear.

When pitching to any media outlet, it's your job to also create an angle that makes your story compelling. If you can craft a narrative and present it well, you greatly increase your chances of getting a story written.

A good press angle makes people react emotionally. If it's not interesting enough to elicit emotion, you don't have a story worth pitching. Furthermore, your story should ideally provoke a specific feeling in readers that makes them want to share the story with others. As Ryan said, "satisfaction is a nonviral emotion"—you want readers to *do* something after reading your piece, not just feel satisfied.

For example, Ryan worked with a client who wrote a book about how Wall Street operates. The book contained technical details about high-frequency stock trading and its impact on the economy. However, when they pitched the story, they focused on the book's implication that the stock market is essentially rigged.

This pitch resulted in much more press than a book about the stock market typically would receive. Rather than leaving it up to reporters to figure out how to position the story, they now had a story "handle" they could grab when writing about the book. This handle created a strong reaction in readers, which drove conversation around the book. If your pitch doesn't draw a line in the sand—with some people shaking their heads and some people nodding—it won't get discussed as widely as you hope.

Ryan offered this template email he's used to pitch reporters successfully:

Subject: *Quick question*

Hey [name],

I wanted to shoot you a note because I loved your post on [similar topic that did a lot of traffic]. I was going to give the following to our publicist, but I thought I would go to you with the exclusive because I read and really enjoy your stuff. My [company built a user base of 25,000 paying customers in two months without advertising / book blows the lid off an enormous XYZ scandal]. And I did it completely off the radar. This means you would be the first to have it. I can write up any details you'd need to make it great. Do you think this might be a good fit?

If so, should I draft something around [their average] words and send it to you, or do you prefer a different process? If not, I totally understand, and thanks for reading this much.

All the best,
[Your Name]

PUBLICITY TACTICS

As we discussed earlier, the best way to get early publicity is to start small. A good first step is using a service like Help A Reporter Out (HARO), where reporters request sources for articles they are working on. While you won't be the centerpiece of the article, assisting a reporter in this way will get you a mention in the piece and help establish your credibility.

Another starting point is to offer reporters commentary on stories related to your industry. One of your many jobs as a startup founder is to stay on top of market trends. If you have a good feel for the pulse of your market, you can send reporters follow-up insights on specific stories. At the same time let them know that you are generally available as an industry source.

You can also use Twitter to reach reporters online. Almost all reporters have Twitter accounts, and you'd be surprised at how few followers many of them have. Just because they're not actively seeking followers, however, doesn't mean they don't have influence. It just means you have a better chance of standing out when you tweet at them.

Staying in contact with reporters over Twitter gives you a leg up when you eventually reach out to them with your more formal pitch. This is exactly how DuckDuckGo was recognized as one of *Time* magazine's top fifty sites in 2011: Gabriel first interacted with the reporter on Twitter and was then included in the feature piece.

Once you have a solid story, you want to draw as much attention to it as you can. Here are a few ways to do it:

- Submit the story to link-sharing sites (reddit, *Hacker News*) with larger audiences.
- Share it on social networks to drive awareness, which you can further amplify with social ads.
- Email it to influencers in your industry for comment. Some of them will share it with their audiences.
- Ping blogs in your space and tell them that you have a story that's getting some buzz. These writers may then want to jump in themselves to cover you.

Once your story has been established as a popular news item, drag it out as long as you can. Email blogs that covered the story (as well as ones that didn't) and offer an interview that adds to the original story. "How We Did This" follow-up interviews are popular.

In addition to driving traffic, publicity can have a substantial impact on your fund-raising efforts. Ryan Holiday talked about this in our interview:

> *PR has a huge impact on early-stage startups. . . . Funding is obviously very important. But funding is essentially gambling. You're saying, "I think this unproven person deserves two million dollars of my money to build a business that may or may not succeed, and if it does succeed we need to find a*

*buyer who will pay even more to take it off our hands." There
are so many things that can go wrong.*

*When people gamble, but they don't tell themselves they're
gambling (as investors do), they need information to justify
their decisions, and they need social proof and examples and
evidence that they're doing the right thing. They already know
if they want to invest in you or not, and they're looking for
confirmation that they made the right call. Press is one of the
single most effective things for pushing people over the edge
and confirming they did the right thing.*

As your startup grows you may choose to hire a PR firm or consultant to help you with this traction channel. This is especially true if you chose to focus on publicity as your core traction channel. A good PR firm can help you:

- Figure out the best messaging and positioning to the press.
- Unify your messaging to the press.
- Do a lot of the legwork in setting up press engagements, especially bigger media tours and events.
- Break into outlets that are traditionally harder to break into, like broadcast TV and radio, where relationships with reporters and producers are harder to form.

However, before making the choice to hire a PR firm, exercise caution. Many of the print reporters we talked to said they ignore almost all pitches from PR firms, but do listen to most founders. PR firms are also expensive: if you're just testing this channel you can often do it faster and cheaper yourself.

TARGETS

- **Focus on the right smaller sites.** Press stories often "filter up," meaning major news outlets are often looking to major blogs for story ideas, which in turn are looking at smaller blogs and forums. That means if you can generate buzz on those sites, you can increase your chances of getting picked up by bigger publications.

- **Build real relationships with the specific reporters covering your startup's market.** Read what they write, comment, offer them industry expertise, and follow them on Twitter.
- **Have newsworthy milestones to share.** Contact reporters only when you can package your milestones into a compelling emotional story. When you do make a pitch, keep it short and sweet!

CHAPTER EIGHT

Unconventional PR

Do you remember Richard Branson wearing a space suit to announce the launch of Virgin Galactic? How about the Old Spice man filming YouTube videos for people who tweeted at him? Or the car service Uber delivering cupcakes and kittens to employees who wanted a break from work? PR stunts like these are not only amusing, but also a proven way to generate press coverage and buzz.

Unconventional PR doesn't suffer from the crowding that the more popular traction channels face. Nearly every company attempts traditional publicity, but few companies focus on stunts and other unconventional ways to get buzz.

There are two different types of unconventional PR. You're probably familiar with the first type: the publicity stunt. A publicity stunt is anything that is engineered to get media coverage. Richard Branson made his press conferences as outlandish as possible (dressing like a woman, driving a tank through the streets) to get the media talking about whatever Virgin was launching. By creating a spectacle around every one of his product launches, Richard Branson turns uninteresting product launches into international headlines.

The second type of unconventional PR is customer appreciation: smaller, more scalable actions (like holding contests or sending handwritten notes to customers) that both increase goodwill as well as generate press coverage. Small gestures like these turn your customers into evangelists, which leads to an increase in organic growth. They also add to your unique image and story, both key elements in building a strong brand.

PUBLICITY STUNTS

When done right, publicity stunts can propel a startup from anonymity to national recognition in an instant. That's exactly what happened to Half.com.

Before their launch, the team at Half.com spent weeks brainstorming ways they could get on the national radar. Eventually, they came up with the unconventional idea to rename a town! And, in one of the most well-executed startup PR stunts, for one year the little town of Halfway, Oregon, was known as Half.com.

Founder Josh Kopelman launched Half.com on the *Today* show with the mayor of Halfway, Oregon. This stunt had everything traditional media loved in a piece: it was unique, surrounded the launch of a high-potential new startup, and told a story about how the company was creating jobs in a small town (they hired several residents).

Half.com received coverage from *The New York Times*, PBS, *The Wall Street Journal*, and hundreds of other publications as a result of this one PR stunt. It launched in late 1999, before the days of ubiquitous email and social media. Even without these sharing tools, this campaign received more than *40 million* impressions and gave Half.com a strong customer base right out of the gate. Just six months later it was acquired for more than $300 million by eBay.

WePay, a Web payments startup, pulled another popular stunt at PayPal's annual developer conference. Rather than marketing to PayPal's customers traditionally, they placed a six-hundred-pound block of ice at the conference entrance.

At the time, PayPal had been criticized for freezing some of its customers' accounts. With this little stunt, WePay shifted the press conversation to focus on these frozen accounts—at PayPal's own conference! This stunt led to thousands of signups. It also put WePay on the map as a viable alternative to PayPal at a time when few people knew it existed.

As another example, DuckDuckGo (Gabriel's search engine) bought a billboard in Google's backyard highlighting its privacy focus. It then used the billboard to get national press stories in *USA Today*, *Wired*, and many other media outlets. The reactions from this stunt alone doubled its user base at the time.

Blendtec is a blender manufacturer located in southern Utah. In 2007, its team decided to create a series of videos called "Will It Blend?" In these videos, Blendtec's CEO stood by one of its blenders and blended items like a rake, golf balls, and even an iPhone.

The series took off shortly after the videos were posted to YouTube. The iPhone video alone has received more than 8 million views, and the "Will It Blend?" series has become one of the one hundred most-viewed on YouTube. All for a company that makes blenders!

Dollar Shave Club, a subscription shaving startup, got similar attention for its launch video titled "Our Blades Are F**king Great." It also has millions of views on YouTube and was the main source of the more than 12,000 customers it acquired within two days of launching. The video was also shared more than 31,000 times on Facebook, received over 9,500 comments, 12,000-plus likes, and more than 16,000 tweets.

The company benefited in other ways as well. Though Dollar Shave Club had been around for just a short while, it quickly ranked third for the Google search "shave." This ranking is largely thanks to the 1,500-plus sites that linked to its video. The video also led to features in *Forbes*, *The Wall Street Journal*, and *Wired*.

CUSTOMER APPRECIATION

On the other end of the unconventional PR spectrum is the more sustainable, systematic form of this traction channel. Customer appreciation is a simple way of saying "be awesome to your customers." The goal is still generating publicity. However, if you fail to get press coverage, you still have happy customers and a stronger, more relatable brand, which significantly increases word-of-mouth effects.

We talked with Alexis Ohanian, founder of reddit and Hipmunk, about how he's made customers fall in love with his companies. Shortly after Alexis launched Hipmunk, a travel booking site, he sent out luggage tags and a handwritten note to the first several hundred people who mentioned the site on Twitter.

These tags were functional, were cute, and led to many tweets and pictures from happy early customers excited to have a chipmunk as a travel companion. Hipmunk also gave out other free items (T-shirts, stickers, handwritten notes) to show its customers' appreciation.

Alexis did the same thing at reddit. In its early days, he handed out free T-shirts with the reddit alien on the front. He personally emailed users to thank them for spending time on the site and did everything he could to make early redditors feel appreciated for being part of the community. These stories became a central theme in reddit's early press articles and had a pronounced effect on the brand.

David Hauser took a similar approach at Grasshopper.com. Over the past several years, he's sent customers Skittles, homemade cookies, Starbucks gift cards, books, and handwritten notes thanking them for their business. Doing these types of things has worked so well for Grasshopper that it has hired two full-time employees whose sole responsibility is to delight customers.

Holding a contest is a great, repeatable way to generate publicity and get some word of mouth. Shopify.com, a popular e-commerce platform, is famous for its annual Build a Business competition (and its six-figure prize). Last year, the contest drove 1,900 new customers and more than $3.5 million in sales on its platform.

Dropbox used to hold a similar contest with its annual Dropquest competition. In Dropquest, users who successfully completed an intellectually challenging online scavenger hunt were rewarded with online recognition,

Dropbox-themed items, and free Dropbox packages for life. In the first year of the competition, almost *half a million* people went through the quest.

Hipmunk has run similar events, like its Mother's Day Giveaway. For this promotion, company staff asked customers to tell them why they love their mothers more than Hipmunk. They received hundreds of submissions via Twitter and sent flowers and chocolates to the moms of the lucky winners. For $500, Hipmunk generated a lot of attention, increased its follower count, and made several customers (and their moms) Hipmunk fans for life.

Hipmunk has run other contests as well, including flying customers home for Thanksgiving and hiring a cartoonist to draw "chipmunked" versions of customers' Facebook profile pictures. For this last promotion, Hipmunk received more than five hundred requests in less than an hour and was covered by *Mashable* and several other popular blogs. Its customers received funny Facebook profile pictures, and Hipmunk once again created a unique connection with its customers and increased its Facebook fans by over 350 percent.

Good customer support is so rare that, if you simply try to make your customers happy, they are likely to spread the news of your awesome product on that basis alone. Zappos is one of the best-known examples of a company that has incredible customer service.

Zappos focuses on creating the best customer experience possible, especially with its support team. In fact, Zappos classifies customer service as a marketing investment, which has interesting implications. For example, if the average time per phone call at Zappos is high, they do not view that as a negative. It might mean that the support team is taking the time necessary to do an outstanding job.

Zappos customer support personnel will help you however they can—whether that's assisting with returns, ordering a pizza, or exchanging workout clothes for a deep fat fryer (real example). With policies like free next-day shipping and free returns, this focus on customer happiness has made Zappos famous among customers who rarely receive such treatment from large companies.

CASE STUDY: DAVID HAUSER

Unconventional PR tactics can have incredible returns on investment. Half.com spent $70,000 and made two hires to generate hundreds of articles and more than 40 million impressions. Dollar Shave Club acquired more than twelve thousand customers with a short video that cost $5,000. Hipmunk received thousands of Facebook likes from a chipmunk-drawing contest that cost the company $500. Blendtec increased its sales by over 500 percent after starting the Will It Blend? series.

David Hauser told us the story of how he and his team rebranded their service as Grasshopper.com. Rather than issue a standard press release, they decided to send chocolate-covered grasshoppers to five thousand influential people! With each package they included a link to a short video about how entrepreneurs can change the world.

After launching the campaign, they received coverage from major news outlets such as Fox News and were the subject of tweets by Guy Kawasaki and Kevin Rose, entrepreneurs with millions of combined Twitter followers. For $65,000, Grasshopper became a well-known brand among entrepreneurs (its target audience). It received major media coverage, created a YouTube video that was viewed more than 200,000 times, was written up in more than 150 blog posts, and increased the number of visitors coming from Twitter and Facebook by over 3,000 percent.

As with Half.com's PR stunt, this Grasshopper 5000 campaign was a result of prolonged brainstorming and careful planning. After its success, the team decided to continue to use unconventional PR as a core channel.

David and his team pulled off another successful stunt when they introduced "The New Dork" video. They noticed a lack of startup-themed viral videos and so parodied the popular Jay-Z and Alicia Keys song "Empire State of Mind" with a video called "The New Dork."

This video received more than 1 million views and was mentioned by Ashton Kutcher, *Mashable*, and *TechCrunch*. The Grasshopper team made a conscious decision to include references to popular publications like *Mashable* in their video. When the video came out, they sent them a quick note about where in the video they made an appearance. This approach gave publications and individuals an incentive to show their audience how cool they were (by referencing themselves in the video) while giving Grasshopper additional exposure.

David's team at Chargify (another one of his startups) pulled off another successful stunt at the popular SXSW conference. Rather than pony up the $10,000 to $15,000 SXSW sponsors normally have to pay, they did something completely different and had a big green bull run around. For $3,000, they hired a stuntman to dress up as Chargify's mascot and get people pumped about Chargify.

Before this conference, Chargify was a virtual unknown. After SXSW attendees saw a green bull giving people high fives, doing backflips, driving a Corvette, and ultimately getting kicked out of the convention center, the Chargify team left the conference with hundreds of customers and a significant jump in brand awareness.

Of course, David's team has also had their share of flops. They've launched unsuccessful March Madness promotions, done failed ticket giveaways, tried to create videos of dancing grasshoppers, and done many other things that just didn't pan out. Even with these flops, this channel has been well worth it to them. David told us that the majority of their marketing expenses are spent on the stunts and unconventional things they do to generate buzz.

TARGETS

- **Do something big, cheap, fun, and original.** A publicity stunt is anything that is engineered to generate a large amount of media coverage. They are often hard to do consistently well, but just one well-executed stunt can move the needle for your company. Publicity stunts need to be creative and extraordinary to succeed. Some types that have been successful repeatedly are competitive stunts and viral videos.
- **Be awesome to your customers and good things follow.** Common ways to do customer appreciation well are through gifts, contests, and amazing customer support. Excelling in

this area is a way to do unconventional PR over a longer period of time.

- **Prepare for failure.** Success in this channel is unpredictable. You should have a defined process for brainstorming and selecting ideas, but also understand that not every idea will work.

CHAPTER NINE
Search Engine Marketing (SEM)

Search engine marketing (SEM) refers to placing advertisements on search engines like Google, where online marketers spend more than $100 million *each day* on Google's AdWords platform. Sometimes the term may also include search engine optimization (SEO), which is a channel we cover separately. In this chapter we just focus on paid search.

Paid search advertising involves buying ads for keyword searches. For example, when someone searches for "leather shoes," a shoe company would bid to show advertisements next to or above the links that organically show up. It's sometimes called "pay-per-click" because the shoe company pays only when a user clicks on an ad.

SEM works well for companies looking to sell directly to their target customer. You are capturing people who are actively searching for solutions.

Here is some basic SEM terminology you should understand before we dive in:

Click-Through Rate (CTR)—the percentage of ad impressions that result in clicks to your site. For example, if one hundred people see your ad and three of them click on it, you have a CTR of 3 percent (3/100).

Cost per Click (CPC)—the amount it costs to buy a click on an advertisement. CPC is the maximum amount you're willing to pay to get a potential customer to your site.

Cost per Acquisition (CPA)—CPA is a measure of how much it costs you to acquire a *customer*, not just a click. For example, suppose you buy clicks at $1 and 10 percent of the people who hit your site after clicking on your ad make a purchase. This puts your CPA at $10:

CPA = $1/10% = $10.

You are paying $10 to acquire each customer. The 10 percent in this equation is known as the *conversion percentage*, which is the rate at which people "convert" by taking the action you want (in this case making a purchase).

For paid search in particular this measure is calculated with the following formula:

CPA = CPC / conversion percentage.

CASE STUDY: INFLECTION

We interviewed Matthew Monahan, CEO and cofounder of Inflection, a company that at its peak was spending six figures *per month* on SEM. Inflection is the company behind Archives.com, a genealogy site, which was acquired by Ancestry.com for $100 million.

Inflection's core technology is its aggregation and management of billions of public records. It originally chose to experiment with SEM because it can provide quick customer feedback and allowed the team to test different product features and messaging. As Matthew told us:

One of the things I want to really emphasize here is just how compelling SEM is as a way to get early customer data in a fairly controlled, predictable manner. So even if you don't expect to be profitable, you can decide to spend $5,000 (or $1,000, or $500) on an advertising campaign and get an early base of customers and users. It informs a whole bunch of things that are really important in terms of the basic [metrics]: conversion rate of your landing pages, how well email captures are working . . . if you're selling a product, what the average cost per customer is and what their lifetime value might be. Having those baseline metrics is critical for informing your strategy moving forward and determining what you need to work on.

The Archives.com team used AdWords to drive traffic to landing pages *before* they made a big investment in building a product. Each landing page was written to test interest in a specific product approach. For example, one page tested "get access to census data" while another tested "get access to your family genealogy." By measuring the CTR for each ad and conversions on the associated landing pages, they determined which product aspects were most compelling to their potential customers and what those people would actually pay for. Matthew explains further:

We just wanted to learn as much as we could for as little cost as possible. So we would test different keyword segments, we would test different concepts. For example, one of the early concepts we were trying to test was whether people wanted to trace their genealogy to find as many of their ancestors as possible. We had to ask ourselves, "Are we trying to build a product experience where you can find hundreds and hundreds of your ancestors, or are we trying to build a product experience where you can go as far back as possible, like trace your family tree all the way back to the 1200s? Or are people more motivated by

*finding out they're related to a celebrity or some historical fig-
ure, and therefore should we focus more on those family trees
and those lineages?"*

Matthew's approach exemplifies the benefits of building traction and
developing your product in parallel. These tests gave the team a clear idea
of the type of product their customers wanted. When they finally built
their product, they built something they *knew* the market would want,
not something they *thought* it would want.

Archives.com's initial SEM campaign broke even after just a few
weeks, meaning their CPA was about equal to the amount of money they
made from each customer. Because they had such positive early results
without even optimizing their landing pages and signup flows, the team
realized that SEM would be a great channel for them. And it was—the
Archives.com business was essentially built on paid search. It dedicated
several employees and more than $100,000 a month to customer acquisi-
tion through this channel.

SEM STRATEGY

The basic SEM process is to find high-potential keywords, group them
into ad groups, and then test different ad copy and landing pages within
each ad group. As data flows in, you remove underperforming ads and
landing pages and make tweaks to better-performing ads and landing
pages to keep improving results.

Google's AdWords is the main platform for SEM because Google
has the most search engine traffic. However, Bing Ads (with its ads running on Yahoo!, Bing, and DuckDuckGo) is also worth looking at. We
will focus on Google's platform here, but the same concepts apply across
all SEM platforms.

Keyword research is the first core component of a strong SEM strategy.
With Google's Keyword Planner, you can discover the top keywords your
target customers use to find products like yours. When you enter a term
in this tool, it tells you how often your keyword (and similar terms) is

searched. Other tools such as KeywordSpy, SEMrush, and SpyFu are valuable for discovering keywords your competition uses to attract customers.

You can further refine this keyword list by adding more qualifying terms to the end of each base term, creating what are known as "long-tail keywords." For example, if you wanted to reach people searching for "census data," you could make that a more targeted search term by adding "1990" to form "1990 census data" or even more long-tail like "1990 Philadelphia census data." Long-tail keywords are less competitive and have lower search volumes, which make them ideal for testing on smaller groups of customers.

Keep in mind that SEM is more expensive for more competitive keywords. As such, you will want to limit yourself to keywords with profitable conversion rates.

After you have keywords you want to target, it's time to run experiments on the AdWords platform. You should not expect your campaigns to be profitable right away. However, if you can run a campaign that breaks even after a short period of time (as Inflection did after a few weeks), then SEM could be an excellent channel for you to focus on.

A campaign is a collection of ads designed to achieve one high-level goal, like selling shoes. You first create different ad groups. For example, if you're an e-commerce store, you might create an ad group for each product type (e.g., sneakers). You then select keywords you want your ad groups to appear for (e.g., "Nike sneakers").

After you've determined the ad groups and keywords you are targeting, create your first ad. When you write an ad, the title should be catchy, memorable, and relevant to the keywords you've paired with it. You will also want to include the keyword at least once in the body of your ad. Finally, you will want to conclude with a prominent call to action (CTA) like "Check out discounted Nike sneakers!"

Once you set up your ads, you should use the Google Analytics URL Builder tool to create unique URLs (Web addresses) that point to your landing pages. These URLs will enable you to track which ads are converting, not just the ones that are receiving the most clicks.

Matthew told us that someone just starting out in this channel should begin testing just four ads. Four ads will give you a good baseline for the performance of SEM as a whole, while still allowing you to test different messaging, demographics, and landing pages.

If a test is promising, you will keep trying to optimize your campaign to make it become profitable. Building a scalable SEM campaign can take a long time because there are so many variables to test—keywords, ad copy, demographic targeting, landing pages, CPC, and more. However, this complexity can actually work to your advantage. As you test and optimize every element of your SEM strategy, you may find opportunities for huge gains. As Matthew told us:

> *I think it's a huge competitive advantage because, even though it can feel like tinkering or incrementalism at the time, what you're really talking about is a major business improvement. Let's say keywords cost 15 cents, and you're running a Web site and for every click you're able to generate 13 cents. Well, if you scale that, that's a losing business. If you improve . . . and you get that 13 cents to 16 cents, now all of a sudden you have something that's more sustainable. And if you go from 16 to 20 cents, you're looking at 25 percent profit margins in terms of sales minus marketing.*
>
> *So a small gain, to go from 13 cents to 20 cents, is essentially a 50 percent gain, but it's a complete game changer in terms of your ability to advertise and your ability to scale a business. And that 50 percent can be achieved through optimizing all of these different levers.*

You can use tools like Optimizely or Visual Website Optimizer to run A/B tests on your landing pages. When we asked Matthew if the approach to SEM he discussed still applied to Inflection as it entered more competitive markets, he said:

> *The fundamental concepts of keyword research, market discovery, running split tests, ad tests, controlling your budget,*

trying to get as close to breaking even as possible, focusing on learning . . . I think those things all still apply. They certainly still apply to us as we build out new keyword segments. That part of the advice doesn't change, even though the dynamics are more competitive.

Each of your ads and ad groups as well as your whole AdWords account has a quality score associated with it. This score is a measure of how well customers are responding to your ads. It includes many factors, from CTR to how long people stay on your site after seeing your ad.

A high quality score can get you better ad placements and better ad pricing. The quality score is Google's way of rewarding advertisers for high-quality advertisements.

Click-through rate has the biggest influence on quality score by a wide margin. Because your ad's relevance to a particular keyword has the biggest impact on your CTR, you should tailor your ads to the keywords they'll appear against, either manually or dynamically (for example by using AdWords' Dynamic Keyword Insertion feature).

Several sources have mentioned that an average CTR for an AdWords campaign is around 2 percent, and that Google assigns a low quality score to ads with CTRs below 1.5 percent. If any of your keywords are getting such low CTRs, rewrite those ads, test them on a different audience, or ditch them altogether.

Inflection makes it a priority to have a strong quality score, which gives it an advantage over less established companies. It also means it has more runway to optimize its ads and conversions.

SEM TACTICS

Once you have a search engine marketing campaign up and running successfully, you may want to start exploring some more advanced tools and features.

When you set up a campaign, you can choose to advertise on the Google search network (traditional paid SEM), the Google content network (ads on non-Google sites), or both. For beginners and for those just testing this traction channel, the content network can be difficult to navigate. Yet once you have established profitable campaigns, you should consider expanding them to the content network, which includes millions of non-Google sites that serve Google's ads.

You should also consider luring people back to your site by retargeting through Google AdWords, or other sites like AdRoll or Perfect Audience. With retargeting, people who visit your site will see your ads elsewhere on the Internet. These ads often convert at a higher rate, as they are aimed at prospects who have already visited your site at least once.

For example, suppose you're a shoe store and a customer put some Nikes in her cart, but didn't complete the checkout process. With retargeting, you could show her an ad for that type of shoe. This personalization makes such ads particularly effective, often generating 3x to 10x higher CTRs.

However, be forewarned that it may feel a little creepy to certain people depending on what data you are using to retarget. People increasingly don't like ads following them around the Internet, especially those that are a reflection of activities they consider personal or private.

Another advanced tool is Google's Conversion Optimizer. It analyzes your conversion tracking data and automatically adjusts your ads to perform better. After you've been running a campaign for a while, using this tool can make your CPAs and keyword targeting better than you would be able to on your own. If you decide to use the Conversion Optimizer, know that it can take time for Google to build a robust prediction algorithm for your campaign.

You can use negative keywords to prevent your ads from showing for certain keywords. You specify words that you *don't* want your ads to appear for: if you're selling eyeglasses, you want to prevent your ads from showing to people who search "wine glasses" or "drinking glasses," as those keywords will convert poorly. This technique can significantly improve your CTRs.

One more advanced tactic is using programming scripts to automatically manage your ads. You might use scripts to set up new ads for certain keywords or to change existing ads. Scripts are especially helpful if you are managing a large number of ads or keywords.

If you're not yet scaling up your efforts or focusing on this traction channel, advanced tactics like these are premature. However, we suggest everyone run some SEM tests because they are straightforward, are cheap to do, and can give you quick insights into your business.

TARGETS

- **Use search engine ads to test product positioning and messaging** (even before you fully build it!). Do not expect your early SEM ad tests to be profitable. If you can run an ad campaign that gets close to breakeven after a few weeks, then SEM could be the traction channel for you to focus on. A test ad campaign can be as little as four ads that you use to experiment.
- **Measure conversions so you can test SEM variables against profitability.** Areas you should be testing include keywords, ad copy, demographic targeting, landing pages, and CPC bids. Cost per acquisition (CPA) is how much it costs you to acquire a customer, and that is ultimately what you need to be testing against.
- **Use longer keywords.** Known as long-tail keywords, they are often less competitive because they have lower search volumes. As such, they are cheaper and so can be more profitable—you just may have to aggregate a lot of them to get the volume you need to move the needle.
- **Pay close attention to your ad quality scores.** High quality scores get you better placement on the page and better pricing on your ads. The biggest factor in quality scores is CTR.

CHAPTER TEN
Social and Display Ads

Display ads are the banner ads that you see on Web sites all over the Internet. Social ads are the ads on social sites, like those in or near your Facebook and Twitter timelines.

Billion-dollar brands such as Rolex, American Apparel, and other household names pay millions each year for social and display ads that push their brands to the forefront of consumers' minds. This is one of the larger traction channels, in which companies spend more than $15 billion a year.

Large display advertising campaigns are often used for branding and awareness, much like offline ads. Display advertising can also elicit a direct response, such as signing up for an email newsletter or buying a product.

Social ads are changing rapidly and are being used for a range of campaigns including both branding and direct response. One application that is unique to social ads and where they have performed exceptionally well is when they are used to build an audience, engage with that audience over time, and eventually convert them into customers.

DISPLAY ADS

Most display advertising is run by ad networks that aggregate advertising inventory across thousands of sites (blogs, communities, media outlets, etc.) and sell that space to advertisers. For advertisers, they can buy ads on multiple sites through a single platform. At the same time, publishers can monetize their content by working with just one partner.

The largest display ad networks are Google's Display Network (also known as the Google content network), Advertising.com (owned by AOL), Tribal Fusion, Conversant, and Adblade. Each of these networks has targeting capabilities that allow you to reach specific types of demographics, and they offer a variety of ad formats like text, image, interactive, and video.

These networks are *enormous*. Google's display network alone has more than 4 *billion* daily page views and 700 *million* monthly visitors, and reaches over 80 percent of the *total* online audience. Mike Colella, founder of Adbeat, an ad intelligence company, told us how display ads allow you to reach a broader audience than SEM ads:

> *The interesting thing about display advertising is that somebody doesn't have to be directly related to whatever your product is to find out about it. For instance, if you're selling some sort of weight-loss product, you don't have to use terms in your display campaign about losing weight. You can use terms relating to nutrition or carbohydrates, because you know if someone starts to read about those things, they have an interest in maintaining or losing weight in some way.*

Niche ad networks focus on smaller sites that fit certain audience demographics, such as dog lovers or Apple fanatics. One such network is The Deck, which targets the niche audience of Web creatives. As an advertiser, you know exactly the audience you're reaching.

Another network, BuySellAds, offers advertisers a self-service platform for buying ads directly from publishers. In addition to buying and selling display advertising, BuySellAds allows advertisers to purchase space on mobile Web sites, Twitter accounts, mobile apps, email newsletters, and RSS feeds. With its flexibility and low starting cost, BuySellAds is an easy way to start testing this traction channel.

The last approach to display advertising is one of the simplest: go directly to site owners and ask to place an ad on their site for a fixed price. This works well when you want to reach the audience of a small site that isn't even running ads. This approach requires only a few emails and a couple hundred dollars.

To get started in display advertising, first understand the types of ads that work in your industry. Tools like MixRank and Adbeat show you the ads your competitors are running and where they place them. Alexa and Quantcast can help you determine who visits the sites that feature your competitors' ads. Then you can determine whether a site's audience is the right fit for you.

SOCIAL ADS

Social ads work especially well for creating interest among potential new customers. People who see these ads may not have any intention of purchasing now—they may not even be familiar with the company or its products. That's okay. The goal of social ads is often awareness oriented, not conversion oriented. A purchase takes place further down the line.

We interviewed Nikhil Sethi, CEO and cofounder of social ad platform Adaptly, to discuss how startups can take advantage of social ads to get traction. Adaptly gives companies one platform to manage and place social ads across many sites. Nikhil told us about the concept of indirect response (as opposed to direct response) in social advertising:

> In the social context, what we're talking about is "indirect response." You're still focused on a sale, an install, a signup, or whatever, but the methodology to get there is different.
>
> Instead of looking at every click and how it converts, indirect response says, "Let's create an environment within

the social context that's geared toward the specific product or
service you're trying to offer, build affinity there, build loyalty
there, and then migrate that audience toward some conver-
sion element we want to occur at a later point in time."

Nikhil's approach may seem counterintuitive. Rather than focusing on selling more product directly (tracking click-through rates, conversions to buying), he believes social advertising works best when you take advantage of the unique characteristics of social media platforms to build an audience. Only after building this audience do you move them toward a conversion—whether through buying, using, or sharing your product.

Building an audience through social ads is more valuable than you might suspect. CareOne, a debt consolidation and relief company, conducted a study in 2011 comparing the customers it received from social ads against those it received from other channels. Here's what it found:

Social media connections filled out the consultation (lead-
generation) form at a 179% higher rate than the typical cus-
tomer. Sales? They were 217% more likely to make their first
payment. For one particular problem area (people who par-
tially fill out the sign-up form then quit), social media pros-
pects went back and completed the form at a 680% higher clip
than non-social media leads. They made their first payment
at an astonishing 732% better rate.

People visit social media sites for entertainment and interaction, not to see ads. An effective social ad strategy takes advantage of this reality. Social ads give companies the opportunity to start a conversation about their products with members of their target audiences.

One way startups can do this is by creating compelling content. Instead of directing people to a conversion page, direct them to a piece of content that explains why you developed your product and your broader mission, or has some other purpose than immediately completing a sale.

As Nikhil told us, this is where social advertising can be extremely effective:

> *If you have a piece of content that has high organic reach, when you put paid [advertising] behind that piece of content the magic happens. As more and more people see it, more and more people engage with it—because it's a better piece of content. . . . Paid is fundamentally only as good as the content you put behind it. And content is only as good as how many people actually see it.*
>
> *Content only goes anywhere if people care about it. . . . With social, it's word of mouth on crack. You should only employ social advertising dollars when you've understood that a fire is starting around your message and you want to put more oil on it. Getting that spark started is based on what you're trying to say: startups do the opposite of this all the time where they waste tens of thousands of dollars trying to push a message that nobody cares about.*
>
> *With social platforms, the burden of success is on the advertiser as opposed to the platform.*

If you've invested time and energy creating a great piece of content, spending a little bit of money to ensure that content gets wide distribution makes sense. At Airbrake, one of the companies Justin ran growth for, they promoted some of their best content on Twitter and Facebook. In one case, after spending just $15 on Twitter ads, they received hundreds of organic retweets, tens of Facebook likes, and two submissions to reddit and *Hacker News*. In total, this $15 drove tens of thousands of visits to Airbrake's site. Just a bit of paid promotion sparked a fire of organic engagement with the content, which was an interview with Stripe's CTO.

This tactic also works well with content distribution networks like Outbrain and Sharethrough. Each of these ad networks promotes your content on popular partner sites like *Forbes*, *Thought Catalog*, *Vice*, *Gothamist*, and hundreds more. These native ad platforms make your content look like any other piece of (native) content on the target site.

Creating engaging social experiences is another way to succeed on social sites. Warby Parker has done this well. They will send you eyeglasses by mail, let you try them on and send them back, all for free. When you receive your glasses, they encourage you to post pictures of yourself to social sites for feedback from others. It is a fun, useful, and engaging process.

Major Social Sites

Here are some well-known social sites where you could advertise.

LinkedIn—LinkedIn's social network is made up of more than 250 million business professionals. LinkedIn ads allow targeting by job title, company, industry, and other business demographics, all factors you can't easily target elsewhere.

Twitter—Twitter also has roughly 250 million users. Twitter's ads come in the form of sponsored tweets that appear in users' feeds. Nikhil mentioned that one of the most effective approaches on Twitter is to turn on paid advertising around real-time events that your audience cares about (e.g., sportswear ads during major sporting events).

Facebook—Facebook has more than one billion active users on its social network. From an advertising perspective, Facebook offers companies the ability to buy targeted ads based on users' interests, pages they like, or even people they're connected with. This granular targeting allows you to target very small groups of people. In fact, Gabriel once ran a test campaign that targeted only his wife! (He targeted her by her alma mater, zip code, and interest affinities, using a picture of their son to see how long it would take for her to notice. Not very long.)

The platform also allows you to reach the larger network of people connected through your fans on Facebook. As Nikhil said:

> *When you buy a Facebook ad, you're buying more than just a targeted fan; you're buying the opportunity to access that fan's social graph. With the proper incentives, fans will share and recommend your brand to their connections.*

StumbleUpon—With more than 25 million "stumblers," Stumble-Upon has a large potential user base looking for new and engaging content. An interesting feature about this site is that ads don't surround the content on StumbleUpon—they *are part of* the content. When people hit the "Stumble" button, they will be directed to a paid piece of content that looks just like any other site on the network.

The downside to traffic from StumbleUpon is that its users are difficult to engage—most users are likely to click off your page as quickly as they came to it. This means you have to make sure to engage these people right away. Blog posts, infographics, and video content can do well on the site.

Foursquare—With more than 45 million users, Foursquare is the largest location-based social network. Foursquare ads can work well if you wish to reach a targeted, local population. Foursquare's ad platform is rapidly evolving but generally allows companies to send out ads hyper-targeted at particular locations or to people who have visited those or similar locations.

Tumblr—Tumblr is all about helping its 100 million–plus users discover high-quality content. Its ad platform allows brands to create and promote sponsored posts, which Tumblr's many users can reblog and engage with.

reddit—With more than 5 billion monthly page views and a thriving platform of more than 175 million monthly uniques, reddit is one of the most popular content sites in the world. reddit ads can take the form of sponsored links that hover at the top of reddit's pages or sponsored ads along the sidebar. The most successful reddit advertisements are controversial or funny. These types of ads encourage redditors (the official name of reddit users) to engage with them by leaving comments and upvoting/downvoting as if they were any other content on the site.

Smart advertisers target communities (there are more than half a million) that are relevant for their product and engage with all the commenters on their ad. As a platform for online communities, the reddit network is vast. Targeting a community of bacon lovers or gay gamers? There are reddit communities for that (r/bacon and r/gaymers, respectively).

YouTube—With more than one billion monthly unique visitors watching more than four billion hours of video, YouTube is by far the world's largest video site. On their platform, brands can create ads that show before a video is played (known as pre-roll) and create banner advertisements on top of videos.

Others—There are plenty of other major sites you can target for social ads—*BuzzFeed*, Scribd, SlideShare, Pinterest, etc. Because these sites were established more recently, advertising on them and even newer ones can offer a unique window of opportunity for substantial growth.

Social ads and display advertising follow similar principles. Namely, you want to understand your audience, experiment with your message, and reach people in a memorable way. They can make sense at any product phase, as they allow for very small or very large ad buys.

TARGETS

- **Contact small sites directly for display ads.** Ask them to run your ads for a small fee. This is an underutilized strategy in display ads, especially in phase I. Study your competitors' ads to get good ideas for A/B tests to run on your ads.

- **Use social ads to build awareness of products and create demand.** The goal with social ads should be to build an audience, engage with that audience over time, and eventually move them to convert to customers. This indirect response strategy usually leads to more conversions than a direct response strategy that tries to get people to convert immediately.

- **Create compelling social content.** The best way to build a presence and engage your audience on social sites is to concentrate on creating less content, but making it highly shareable. When your content is getting naturally shared, that's the time to promote it further with social ads.

CHAPTER ELEVEN
Offline Ads

E ven today, advertisers spend more on offline ads than they do on online. There are many kinds of offline ads—TV, radio, magazines, newspapers, yellow pages, billboards, and direct mail. All of these can be utilized at almost any scale, from local campaigns to national ones. They are used by billion-dollar brands like Walmart and by local teens looking for babysitting gigs.

The demographics of each advertising medium are the most important factor to consider when making an offline ads purchase. For example, ads in the classified section of a newspaper will appeal primarily to an older crowd that still buys newspapers. You'll want to think about location, gender, race, age, income, and occupation—and how each matches up with your target audience.

You should be able to answer many of these questions by asking for an audience prospectus (sometimes called an ad kit) from whatever company is selling the ad inventory. As an example, for billboards you should receive information about the aggregate demographics of the area around the billboard, approximately how many people drive by it per day, and a sense of who those people are.

Many kinds of offline outlets allow you to go even further and pick not just the demographics, but also the mind-set of the customer you're approaching. In this case you're also taking aim at a sensibility. The kinds of people who read a local arts magazine represent a different sensibility from the people who listen to the local top-40 music station.

One way to find the best offline places to advertise is to ask your target customers. What magazines do they read, or radio stations do they listen to? Where do they see ads they actually remember?

OFFLINE ADS STRATEGY

In general, the cost of an offline ad depends on its reach. A billboard in Times Square goes for much more than one in the middle of Ohio because more people see it. Most offline advertisements work similarly.

Thanks to the wide variety of offline media available, you can scale your ad buys according to your budget and product phase. Not sure if magazine ads will be a good channel for you? Buy a small ad in a niche publication and give it a test. Want to see if newspapers reach your audience effectively? Buy a few advertisements in a local paper. For as little as $300, you can put out a radio ad in a market you're targeting and see how it performs. Billboards are the same way: you can buy space on one for a few hundred bucks a month.

Once you've established that offline ads are effective, you can save money by signing a longer advertising contract. With an up-front commitment, advertisers will give you a substantial discount.

To get really cheap offline ads, look for remnant advertising. Remnant advertising is ad space that is currently being unused. For example, publications accept almost any price when selling empty inventory near print deadlines: after all, it is a complete loss for them if they don't sell that space. Tim Ferriss, bestselling author of *The 4-Hour Body* and *The 4-Hour Workweek*, has said this on the subject:

If dealing with national magazines, consider using a print or "remnant ad" buying agency such as Manhattan Media or Novus Media that specializes in negotiating discounted pricing of up to 90% off rate card. Feel free to negotiate still lower using them as a go-between.

If you're not sensitive to location or timing, you can get substantial discounts by committing to buy remnant inventory. This can be a cheap and effective strategy to reach millions of people if you have a mass-market product. Think of those "We buy ugly houses" billboards or any of the repetitive billboards that you see all over the place: they are likely using this approach.

Offline ads are much harder to track as compared with online ads that have tracking built in. Successful offline tracking involves the use of unique Web addresses and promotional codes to measure effectiveness. For example, we could create flyers that link to tractionbook.com/flyer. By tracking visits to that specific URL, we could approximate how many visits originated from our flyer campaign.

There are other tracking options as well. Jason Cohen, founder of code review company Smart Bear Software, was doing all kinds of offline advertising—magazines, trade shows, newspapers, and more—to sell his software. When people signed up, Jason included a section that asked new customers, "How did you hear about us?" This question was designed to measure the efficacy of the company's online and offline campaigns.

Jason also included an offer for a free book on code review in Smart Bear ads. This book offer was another way to track the effectiveness of the ads. If an ad in *Dr. Dobb's Journal* resulted in a high number of book orders, then there was a high probability that the promotion worked.

PRINT ADVERTISING

Print advertising encompasses magazines, newspapers, the yellow pages, flyers, direct mail, and local directories. Among the different categories of offline ads, print trails only TV in terms of overall spending. Print advertising is appealing because it works with just about any budget and allows for precise audience targeting.

There are nearly seven thousand different magazines in the United States, ranging from commercial publications with millions of subscribers to small trade publications with hundreds of readers.

There are three general magazine categories: consumer publications that appeal to the larger population (these are the ones you see on newsstands and in grocery stores), trade publications covering a particular industry or business, and local magazines that you'll see for free along sidewalks and near grocery stores.

You need to understand the reader demographics, circulation, and publication frequency of any magazine you're considering. To get this information, just ask the magazine for its ad kit (also known as a media package, media kit, or press kit).

No matter how well you've targeted your audience, your magazine ad will not get a good response unless it is well designed. A compelling magazine ad will have an attention-grabbing header, an eye-catching graphic, and a tagline or description of the product's benefits. Jason Cohen mentioned that the Smart Bear ads that performed well all had a strong call to action: in his case, the offer for that free book.

Newspapers share many characteristics with magazines. They are published on both a national and local scale, their pricing is largely based on the circulation of a given paper, and they allow you to choose the type of ad you want in the paper. One major difference, however, is that newspapers slant heavily toward the over-thirty demographic. Many young people still buy magazines. Not many young people still buy newspapers offline.

There are some ad campaigns that are uniquely suited to a newspaper setting. A few examples are time-sensitive offers (as for events or sales), awareness campaigns (often as part of a larger marketing effort across multiple channels), and widely publicized announcements (as for product launches).

Direct mail entails any printed advertising message (ads, letters, or catalogs) delivered to a specific group of consumers through the postal system.

It may surprise you to learn how effectively you can target customers through direct mail. You can build up a list of customers on your own or buy a list from a mailing organization. Simply do a Web search for "direct mail lists" to find companies selling such information. Beware that buying lists can be perceived as spammy, and can be a complete waste of money if they are untargeted.

You can buy lists grouped by demographic, geography, or both. These lists often sell for about $100 for one thousand consumer names, and a bit more for business names and addresses. There are even direct mail services that will buy address lists, print your marketing materials, and assemble and mail everything for you. This makes sense if you're planning to do a high-volume mailing—otherwise, you're the one who has to do the printing, addressing, and mailing.

Here are a few good tactics to use if you are interested in pursuing direct mail:

- If doing a postal direct-response campaign, provide a self-addressed envelope to increase the number of recipients who respond.
- Use handwritten envelopes and cards to increase the chances of someone opening and reading your mailing.
- Have a clear action you want the recipient to take, such as visiting your Web site, coming into your store, buying a certain product, or signing up for an email list.
- Investigate bulk mail with the postal service to get reduced pricing.

Local print ads include buying space in local flyers, directories, calendars, or publications such as church bulletins, community newsletters, or coupon booklets. These print ads are a good way to test print advertising because of their modest cost: just a few hundred dollars can expose you to thousands of people in a targeted area. Ads in the yellow pages are similarly inexpensive.

Unorthodox strategies like hanging flyers in areas where your potential customers visit can be a surprisingly effective way to get some early traction for your company. For example, InstaCab hired cyclists to bike around San Francisco and hand out business cards to people who were trying to hail taxis. These were well targeted (it's a good bet that someone hailing a taxi would appreciate an easier way of getting around) and got the company some good buzz and customer adoption early on.

OUTDOOR ADVERTISING

If you want to buy space on a billboard, you'll probably contact one of three companies: Lamar, Clear Channel, or Outfront Media. They are the power players in this $6 billion industry. If you want to get a sense of what is available in a given area, go to the Web sites of the above companies and contact a local representative. They will give you PDFs of local available billboards, showcasing their locations and audience.

We have some personal experience with billboard advertising, as we discussed in the publicity chapter. Gabriel strategically placed a billboard in the startup-heavy SoMa district of San Francisco to call out the differences between the privacy practices of Google and DuckDuckGo.

A startup search engine calling out the big guy in their backyard—that is the kind of strong message that can get you some traction. In this case, DuckDuckGo didn't just capture the attention of the people who drove by the billboard. It also got press coverage from *Wired, USA Today, Business Insider,* and several other blogs and media outlets. That month, DuckDuckGo's user base doubled!

What does all this cost? Gabriel's billboard cost $7,000 for a month. Billboards in less prominent locations can cost anywhere between $300 and $2,500 per month. Ads in Times Square, on the other hand, can run you $30,000 to $100,000 per month.

The cost of billboard space depends on the size of the ad, where it is located, the number of impressions your ad can provide, and the type of billboard it is (e.g., digital). Every billboard has an advertising score, known as a GRP score (Gross Ratings Points), based on the above factors. The number of potential impressions is based on the number of people in an area who could see the billboard: a full score means that a given billboard should reach 100 percent of the driving population during a month.

The major downside of billboard advertising is that it is difficult for people to take immediate action on what they see. It is dangerous for someone to visit a Web site, call a number, or buy a product while driving on a highway. However, billboards are extremely effective for building awareness around events—concerts, conferences, or other activities coming to an area. In Las Vegas, for example, you'll see billboards touting acts and musicians performing in the coming weeks.

Transit ads are placed in or on buses, taxis, benches, and bus shelters. Most ads of this kind can be effective as a direct-response tool because people in transit are a captive audience.

If you want to get started with transit advertising, we suggest checking out a company that specializes in these ads, like Blue Line Media. These media agencies can help you figure out where to advertise, how to create a memorable transit ad, and how to best measure and optimize such a campaign.

Another advantage of billboards and transit media is that they are replaced only when there are new ads to go up. While a radio, TV, or print ad will run only once, there's always a chance your billboard will stay up long past the dates you paid for.

RADIO AND TV ADVERTISING

Radio ads are priced on a cost-per-point (CPP) basis, where each point represents what it will cost to reach 1 percent of the radio station's listeners. The higher the CPP, the more it will cost you to run an ad on a station.

This cost also depends on which market you're advertising in, when your commercials run, and how many ads you've bought with that station. To give you an idea of what a radio ad costs, an ad running on a station for a week is often $500 to $1,500 in a local market and up to $4,000 to $8,000 in a larger market like Chicago. If you are scaling your radio buys, satellite radio is another place to consider. With more than 50 million subscribers, SiriusXM can help you reach a lot of people with just one advertising relationship.

TV advertisements are often used as branding mechanisms. Most of us remember famous Nike, Apple, or Wendy's commercials. When you consider that 90 percent of consumers watch TV, and the average adult watches twenty-six hours of TV per week, this is an offline channel that must be considered.

Quality is critical for TV ads. Production costs for actors, video equipment, editing, sound, sound effects, and shooting can run to tens of thousands of dollars. In fact, some of the higher-end commercials you'll see can cost upward of $200,000 to make.

Fortunately, there are ways for you to reduce the costs of creating a TV ad. Using animation as opposed to live actors is a lot cheaper. If you do use live actors, you can recruit local film students to perform for you. Finally, just keeping the commercial as simple as possible will go a long way toward reducing costs.

In addition to the cost of creating an ad, there is the (national average) $350,000 for actual airtime. These costs make national TV campaigns tough to swallow for many small startups. However, over the last few years it's become possible to advertise on TV without spending so much money.

Local TV spots on one of the 1,300-plus TV stations in the United States can be an effective and reasonably priced way to make an impression. Prices for local commercials can range from $5 to $50 per one thousand viewers for a thirty-second time slot. As with so many other offline channels, you just have to contact the station to find out the number of viewers a station has and how much a TV spot costs.

Buying TV ads is a rather opaque process that involves a lot of negotiation, as there are no rate cards in the industry like those in print advertising. Thus, for larger media buys, you will likely want to hire a media buyer or agency to handle the many sellers out there and to ensure that you get a quality spot at a fair price.

Infomercials are basically long-form TV advertisements. You've probably seen them, from the Snuggie to ShamWow, and all sorts of knives, vacuums, and workout products. Though the products and pitchmen in them frequently become punch lines, infomercials can work surprisingly well. For example, they were the main growth engine behind the rise of P90X and its $400 million in sales.

Traditionally, products in the following categories have used infomercials to gain serious traction:

- Workout equipment or programs
- Body care products
- Household products (kitchen, cleaning)
- Vacuum cleaners
- Health products (e.g., juicers)
- Work-from-home businesses

Products like these require more time to showcase what they have to offer. Consider the Snuggie. In a fifteen-second spot, it'd be really difficult to sell you on why the Snuggie is a great product. But through two-minute shorts, the Snuggie was able to sell millions of units.

Infomercials can cost anywhere between $50,000 and $500,000 to make. They can be two-minute infomercial shorts or the more traditional twenty-eight-minute episodes. These ads are almost always direct response: advertisers want people to see it, then visit a Web site or call in to take advantage of a special offer. The best infomercial marketers will often test their messaging, calls to action, and bonuses by running radio ads in advance, seeing what works well, and then incorporating those bonuses and messages into their commercial.

CONCLUSION

Clearly, there are lots of ways to take advantage of offline advertising. The branding potential, cost, impact, and flexibility of this channel make it a really strong one to consider when looking at how to get traction in later phases.

The best way to approach this channel is to understand that there is no guaranteed way to predict what will work. But, if you keep at it, you may end up with an effective offline advertising strategy. As Jason Cohen said:

> *One thing I learned at Smart Bear is that I have zero ability to predict what's going to work. There'd be a magazine where I thought, "This is just some piddly magazine, surely no one reads this," and sure enough it was cheap (due to small circulation) and it'd do terrifically! Our ROI on some of those were incredible. And you just couldn't predict, whether on circulation size or media type, how it was going to go. And it changed over time—an ad might be good for a quarter, or a year, and then decay slowly until it wasn't valuable anymore. It was unpredictable and decayed over time: so the only thing we were left with was trying everything and measuring what worked.*

TARGETS

- **Run cheap tests by first targeting local markets.** It is hard to predict what will work, so it is often useful to run several small offline ad tests in parallel. Each offline ad medium is testable locally. Then you can scale up to regional or national campaigns if warranted.
- **Seek out remnant ad inventory for the highest discounts.** You can use remnant ads for both initial tests and scaling this channel. The downside is less targeting ability, both in terms of demographics and timing.
- **Use unique codes or Web addresses to track the effectiveness of different offline ad campaigns.** Make sure before you set up tests or campaigns that you can trace conversions back to specific offline ads.

CHAPTER TWELVE
Search Engine Optimization (SEO)

Almost all Internet users turn to search engines for answers. Search engine optimization (SEO) is the process of improving your ranking in search engines in order to get more people to your site. As Rand Fishkin, founder of the popular SEO software company Moz, told us:

> At its base, SEO is starting with a content strategy and finding a way to attract relevant visitors through search engines. You have to intelligently design this kind of [content] and make sure search engines can find and rank that content.

SEO allows you to amplify all of the good things you're already doing in other traction channels (publicity, unconventional PR, content marketing) and use them to bring in more customers from search engines. Though competitive, SEO can scale well at any phase, often at low cost.

SEO STRATEGY

The most important thing to know about SEO is that the more high-quality links you have to a given site or page, the higher it will rank. If you're new to SEO, we recommend starting with the *Moz Beginner's Guide to SEO* to learn the fundamentals. These include making sure you're using the keywords you want to target appropriately on your pages, like in your page titles and headings.

Instead of these more obvious basics, we'll head straight to specific strategies and tactics. In SEO, there are two high-level strategies to choose from: fat head and long tail. Let us first explain these strange names.

Consider all the searches that people make, sorted by the number of times that search is made. At the top are one- and two-word searches like "Dishwashers," "Braves," and "Facebook." They make up about 30 percent of all searches. The other 70 percent are longer searches that don't get searched as much, but in the aggregate add up to the majority of searches made.

If you graph all these searches by the number of times they are made, the first 30 percent get clumped at the front and the last 70 percent make up a long tail, because many of those are searched only a few times. These latter searches are called "long-tail" keywords because they make up this long tail. Oppositely, those searches that are searched a lot and clumped at the front are called "fat-head" keywords.

A fat-head strategy involves trying to rank for search terms that directly describe your company. For example, a toy company that specializes in wooden toys might try to rank for "wooden toys." These are all fat-head keywords.

On the other hand, a long-tail strategy involves trying to rank for more specific terms with lower search volumes. That same toy company might try to rank for searches in that long tail like "poisonous chemicals in wooden toy blocks" or "wood puzzles for 3 year olds." Again, even though these searches have lower volumes, in the aggregate they account for the majority of all searches.

When determining which strategy to use, you should keep in mind that the percentage of clicks you get drops off dramatically as you rank lower on a search results page. Only about 10 percent of clicks occur beyond the first ten links, so you want to be as high up on the first page as possible. Your ability to rank high on the first page should be a deciding factor in deciding whether to pursue a particular SEO strategy.

Fat-head Strategy

To determine if a fat-head SEO strategy is worthwhile, first research what terms people use to find products in your industry, and then see if the search volumes are large enough to move the needle. Google currently provides a useful tool for this process called Keyword Planner (part of Google AdWords). You can type in search terms that describe your products and then see the search volumes for these terms. You can also get keywords by looking at your competitors' Web sites and seeing what words they use in their home page titles and headers.

You want to find terms that have enough volume such that if you captured 10 percent of the searches for a given term then it would be meaningful. You don't want to spend resources ranking for a fat-head term that gets only two hundred searches per month. Sometimes you cannot find any good terms because your product category is so new that there is no search demand for it yet. Rand used Uber as an example:

> *The problem with Uber is that there's not a lot of search demand for it. I mean nobody searches for "alternatives to taxicabs that I can hire via my phone." It's just not a thing. And this is a problem with a lot of startups that are essentially entering a niche where nothing had existed previously. . . . There's just not search volume.*

The next step is determining the difficulty of ranking high for each term. Using tools like Open Site Explorer, examine the number of links competitors have for a given term. This will give you a rough idea of how difficult it will be to rank high. If a competitor has thousands of links for a term you want to rank for, just realize it will likely take lots of focus on building links and optimizing for SEO to rank above them.

Next, take steps to narrow your list of targeted keywords to just a handful. Go over to Google Trends to see how your keywords have been doing. Have these terms been searched more or less often in the last year? Are they being searched in the geographic areas where you're seeking customers?

You can further test keywords by buying SEM ads against them. If these ads convert well, then you have an indication that SEO could be a strong growth channel using these keywords.

Now you're at the implementation stage of fat-head strategy. Orient your site around the terms you've chosen. If you are an accounting software site and "small business accounting software" is your main term, include that phrase in your page titles and home page.

Finally, get other sites to link to your site, ideally using the exact terms you want to rank for. For example, an article may read something like "XYZ Company releases version of small business accounting software" (where an underline denotes the link). Exact matches give you a significant boost, and also links from higher-quality sites matter more.

Long-Tail Strategy

The majority of searches conducted through search engines are "long-tail" searches. These are longer terms that are highly specific—things like "gluten free for arthritis" or "private search engine." Individually, searches for these terms don't amount to much: together, though, they make up 70 percent of all searches.

Because it is difficult to rank high for competitive (fat-head) terms, a popular SEO strategy for early-stage startups is to focus on the long tail. With this strategy, you bundle long-tail keywords together to reach a meaningful number of customers.

As with the fat-head strategy, the Google Keyword Planner is the first way to evaluate whether a long-tail strategy may be effective for you. But this time you are seeking information on more specific, long-tail terms. What are search volumes for a bunch of long-tail keywords in your industry? Do they add up to meaningful amounts?

A second way to evaluate a long-tail strategy is to look at the analytics software you have on your site (such as Google Analytics or Clicky). These applications will tell you some of the search terms people are using to get to your site right now. If you are already naturally getting a significant amount of traffic from long-tail keywords, then this strategy might be a good idea.

If you do not have any content that is drawing people to your site via long-tail keywords, you have two choices. First, you could create some Web pages, and then after a few months check your analytics. Second, you could look at competitors' Web sites to determine whether they are getting meaningful long-tail SEO traffic. Here are signs that they are:

- They have a lot of landing pages. You can see what types of pages they are producing by searching site:domain.com in a search engine. For example, if I wanted to see how many landing pages Moz has created targeting long-tail keywords, I could search site:moz.com and get a sense of how many landing pages they have.
- Check out Alexa search rankings and look at the percentage of visitors your competitors are receiving from search. If you look across competitors and one site receives a lot more visitors from search than others, you can guess they are using some kind of SEO strategy.

If you proceed with a long-tail SEO strategy, its success will boil down to your being able to produce significant amounts of quality content. Patrick McKenzie, founder of Bingo Card Creator and Appointment Reminder, told us how he approaches doing so:

> You build a machine that takes money on one end and spits rankings out the other. For example, with Bingo Card Creator I pay money to a freelancer to write bingo cards with associated content about them that get slapped up on a page

on the Web site. Because those bingo cards are far too niche for any educational publisher to target, I tend to rank very well for them.

For ten to twenty dollars per search term, you can pay someone to write an article that you won't be embarrassed to put on your Web site. For many SaaS [Software as a Service] startups, the lifetime value of a customer at the margin might be hundreds or thousands of dollars. So they [articles and landing pages] don't need much traffic at all on an individual basis to aggregate into a meaningful number to the business.

The reason my business works is fundamentally because this SEO strategy works phenomenally well.

In our interview, Patrick told us about his Owls of East Asia bingo cards. He uses a landing page that specifically discusses owls of East Asia and has a custom bingo card template just for this long-tail topic. This page has resulted in about $60 worth of business over three years. With a $3.50 content creation cost, it was an investment worth making. It works because few other sites on the Internet have a page specifically for people searching "owls of East Asia bingo." In Patrick's case, hundreds of these sorts of $3.50 investments with $60 to $100 returns add up to big profits.

Patrick has built up a series of subpages on his site, each of which targets a bucket of keywords he wants to rank for. For example, there's the bingo card category for "plants and animals." This category includes pages like "dog breeds bingo," "cat breeds bingo," and (of course) "owls of East Asia bingo." For each of these subpages, he hired a freelancer to research the term and create a unique set of bingo cards and associated landing pages.

You can implement this tactic by designing a standard landing page with some basic content and a simple layout structure. Then use oDesk or Elance to find freelancers willing to churn out targeted articles for long-tail topics that your audience is interested in.

Another way to approach long-tail SEO is to use content that naturally flows from your business. To evaluate whether you could use this tactic, ask yourself: what data do we collect or generate that other people may find useful?

Large businesses have been built this way: Yelp, TripAdvisor, and Wikipedia have all gained most of their traffic by producing automated long-tail content. This tactic was also the main channel for Gabriel's last startup, Names Database. When people searched for old friends and classmates, they would come across the Names Database page of the individual they were searching for. These pages were automatically generated from the data that was naturally gathered by the product. After search engines indexed them, these pages sent a great deal of organic traffic from individuals doing long-tail searches for individual names.

Sometimes this data is hidden behind a login screen and all you need to do is expose it to search engines. Other times you may need to be more creative about aggregating data in a useful manner. For example, if you want to reach individuals searching for "foreclosed homes," creating landing pages based on geography might work well. This means generating pages matching searches like "recently foreclosed homes in Queens, New York City."

SEO TACTICS

Whether you pursue a fat-head or long-tail strategy, SEO comes down to two things: content and links. The more aligned your content is with the keywords it's targeting, the better it will rank. Similarly, the more links you can get from credible and varying sources, the better your rankings.

Getting links is often more difficult because it involves people outside of your company. Here are some ways to build links:

- **Publicity**—when you are covered by online publications, reporters will link to your Web site.
- **Product**—with some products, you can produce Web pages as part of your product that people naturally want to share. A great example is LinkedIn profile pages.

- **Content marketing**—creating strong, relevant content that people want to read, and thus share.
- **Widgets**—giving site owners useful things to add to their sites, which also contain links back to yours.

There is a difference between creating amazing content that spreads like wildfire and hiring freelancers to write boilerplate articles for long-tail keywords. Both are valid strategies (and can work well in tandem), but there is a big difference in quality. The high-quality content is useful in natural link building, especially for fat-head strategies.

Rand suggests using infographics, slideshows, images, and original research to drive links, as these are all things people naturally share. Since the end goal is to get links, you'll want to specifically target people who will link back to you. This group of people will vary depending on the product, but in general people who run blogs are big social sharers. Reporters are usually good targets as well.

Remember, links are the dominant factor in a site's ranking for a given term. Open Site Explorer can tell you how many links you are getting and where they are coming from. You can also look at your competitors' link profiles to get ideas of other places to target for link building.

In SEO, there are a few big don'ts. The biggest: don't buy links. Buying links is against search engine guidelines and companies get heavily penalized for doing so. Similarly, trying to trick search engines in any way can lead to serious ranking penalties.

These sketchy tactics are referred to as "black-hat," as opposed to "white-hat" or "gray-hat" (on or close to the line). You want to stay squarely in the "white-hat" arena.

To be clear, black-hat tactics can work in the short term, and therefore can seem quite attractive. However, it is hard to build a long-term sustainable business on them because at some point search engines will crack down on them and you'll lose traffic due to penalization.

CONCLUSION

SEO is one of the cornerstones of what is commonly referred to as "inbound marketing." Inbound marketing brings customers inbound, from things like social media and SEO. Rand told us that Moz gets 85 percent of its customers inbound. Mike Volpe from HubSpot said something similar:

> *Today we have 30 people in marketing and 120 in sales, all based in Cambridge, MA (no outside sales) and we attract 45–50k new leads per month, 60–80 percent of which are from inbound marketing (not paid). The inbound leads are 50 percent cheaper and close 100 percent more than paid leads.*
>
> *My personal experience and industry knowledge tells me that most other SaaS [Software as a Service] companies get more like 10 percent of their leads from inbound marketing, and generate 2–5k leads per month in total, whereas we get 70–80 percent of our leads from inbound and we generate 45,000+ new leads per month.*

TARGETS

- **Find search terms that have enough search volume to move the needle for your company.** If you can't find enough search volume, or can't rank high for those terms, SEO won't be a great strategy for your business. If you identify some terms that could work, you can further qualify them by running search ads against them to test whether they actually convert customers.
- **Generate long-tail landing pages by using cheap freelancers.** Or, if your product can naturally produce good long-tail content, use it to create the landing pages yourself.
- **Focus on how you will build links.** Whether you pursue a fat-head or long-tail strategy, SEO comes down to two things: content and links. Link building is often the more

challenging of the two. Creating amazing content is one way to quickly build links.

- **Avoid "black-hat" SEO tactics that violate search engine guidelines, especially buying links.** These banned tactics will eventually come back to bite you.

CHAPTER THIRTEEN
Content Marketing

Think back to the last few Web sites you've used and take a look at their blogs. In all likelihood, they're infrequently updated and have few comments or, worse, are frequently updated and an avalanche of boring.

Compare that experience to reading a well-known company blog like those of Moz, Unbounce, or OkCupid. They write posts that receive hundreds of comments, lead to major publicity, and result in thousands of shares. This massive engagement leads to massive growth. In fact, for each of these companies its blog was at one time its largest source of customer acquisition.

For this traction channel, we spoke with two successful entrepreneurs who have very different approaches toward content creation. Rick Perreault, founder and CEO of Unbounce, told us how Unbounce started using its blog as a marketing platform the day it started building its application. In fact, Unbounce began blogging a year before it even had a product! Unbounce's blog raised its profile in the online marketing industry and is still its main source of traction.

On the other end of the spectrum, we talked with Sam Yagan, cofounder of OkCupid. The popular online dating service launched in 2004 but didn't start seriously blogging until 2009. Though it focused on other traction channels early on, OkCupid really started to take off when it focused on content marketing.

CASE STUDY: UNBOUNCE

As we discussed earlier, many startups fall into the product trap—building a product before thinking about distribution. Unbounce, a company that provides simple landing page creation software, successfully avoided this trap. Literally from day one, founder Rick Perreault began sketching out the product features for Unbounce on the company blog. Rick's first hire was actually a full-time blogger! As he said:

> If we had not started blogging at the beginning the way we did, Unbounce would not be here today. . . . Our content still drives customers. Something we wrote in January 2010 still drives customers today. Whereas if I had spent money on advertising in January, that's it. That money is spent. If you invest in content, it gets picked up by Google. People find it, they share it, and it refers customers almost indefinitely.
>
> By the time we launched in the summer of 2010, we were doing twenty thousand unique visitors per month to the blog. . . . It was up and running for almost a year before we launched.
>
> Now our blog is our primary source of customer acquisition. People write about Unbounce. Other people tweet about our posts. . . . Our blog is the centerpiece of all our marketing.

This blog-from-the-beginning approach allowed Unbounce to launch with an email list over five thousand strong. This wasn't your typical startup product launch.

The Unbounce team relied heavily on social media to drive readers to their blog. After every post they wrote, they'd ping influencers on Twitter asking for feedback. They also engaged with their target customers by writing useful answers on targeted forums like Quora. Though actions like these may not scale, they're okay when getting started because you're building toward a point where your content will spread on its own. That's exactly what happened with Unbounce, and eventually its content started spreading more organically.

Unbounce further capitalized on its blog traffic by giving away free infographics and e-books to grow its email list. This meant that when it finally opened up its product beta, Unbounce could email its list and launch successfully.

Getting to this point wasn't as easy as it might seem. Even with awesome biweekly posts about online marketing, it took six months for the Unbounce team to see significant results from their blog. However, once they captured this significant audience, they never looked back.

CASE STUDY: OKCUPID

OkCupid is one of the most popular online dating sites in the United States and was acquired by Match.com for a reported $50 million. OkCupid approached its blog differently from Unbounce, making it the core traction channel only after five years of being in business. Sam Yagan told us that once they launched the blog in 2009, growth increased rapidly.

Much like Unbounce, OkCupid's blog was the focal point of all its marketing activities. Unlike Unbounce, the OkCupid team wrote longer posts with less frequency. Each of OkCupid's posts took a month to write and drew on the data they had from studying the usage patterns of their members. They intentionally wrote controversial posts (e.g., "How Your Race Affects the Messages You Get") to generate traffic and conversation.

Because OkCupid was a *free* online dating site, it couldn't afford to pay much to acquire customers—in fact, it never did any sort of paid advertising. This meant that traction channels without per-user acquisition costs (e.g., publicity, content marketing, SEO, viral marketing) needed to drive all of its growth.

Interestingly, the OkCupid team received much more organic publicity after launching the blog than they did when working with PR firms. CNN, Rachael Ray, *The New York Times,* and many other media outlets were interested in the blog topics they covered.

Their blog also had major SEO benefits. When they launched it, they were nowhere near the top of search results for the term "online dating." About a year later, they were the first result for that highly competitive term.

CONTENT MARKETING TACTICS

The most common hurdle in content marketing is writer's block. To overcome it, simply write about the problems facing your target customers. Presumably, you know more about the industry you're working in than your potential customers. This means that you should be able to provide insight on subjects they care about.

Every single industry has issues people struggle with. In Unbounce's case, they wrote posts about landing page optimization, PPC (pay-per-click) conversions, and so on. OkCupid's posts, such as "Exactly What to Say in Your First Message," addressed the concerns of online dating users in an entertaining way.

Unbounce found that infographics are shared about twenty times more often than a typical blog post and have a higher likelihood of getting picked up by other online publications. For example, in 2012 Unbounce released the "Noob Guide to Online Marketing." This infographic drove tens of thousands of downloads and thousands of paying customers. One year later it was still shared on Twitter about once an hour.

Most marketers fail to realize that quality is no substitute for quantity. Both Rick and Sam made it a point to say there's no shortcut to creating quality content. If what you're writing isn't useful, it doesn't matter how hard you try to spread your content on Twitter. It just won't spread.

The secret to shareable content is showing readers they have a problem they didn't know about, or at least couldn't fully articulate. A solution is nice, but it's not as good for drawing in readers as showing them they've been going about some aspect of their life all wrong.

In the early days, it's unlikely that your blog will see much traffic, regardless of content quality. Even Unbounce was receiving less than eight hundred monthly visits after six months of consistently putting out good content. It took awhile longer for the blog to grow to twenty thousand monthly visitors.

Fortunately, there are ways to build momentum faster. Unbounce engaged in any online forum where conversations were taking place about online marketing, and did its best to contribute. It was particularly successful reaching out to influential people on Twitter. It would simply follow marketing mini-celebrities and ask them for feedback on recent posts.

One of the best methods of growing your audience is guest posting. This tactic is especially powerful in the early days when you essentially have no audience to work with yourself. Unbounce started doing guest posts on other popular blogs after just three months of blogging on its own.

As you move forward, monitor social mentions and use analytics to determine which types of posts are getting attention and which are not. Many bloggers are surprised at which posts do well. That is a good reason to keep a regular content schedule: it can be hard to anticipate what exactly will resonate with your audience.

CONCLUSION

Quick: name three venture capitalists or ask your startup friends to do so. Many people will mention Fred Wilson, Brad Feld, or Mark Suster. Why? Because they have popular blogs. There are plenty of other great venture capitalists who do not have similar brand recognition.

One of the best things about this traction channel is how it positions you as a leader in your space. Unbounce and OkCupid are both great examples of how a popular blog can make a company a recognized industry leader in a highly competitive space.

Recognition as a primary voice in an industry leads to opportunities to speak at major conferences, give press quotes to journalists, and influence industry direction. It also means your content is shared many more times than it would be otherwise.

For Unbounce, some of the biggest benefits of having a strong company blog came in the form of comarketing opportunities. When they were just starting out, they tried contacting popular companies to arrange partnerships. These types of business development pitches were ineffective early on, but that changed after their blog started getting readership. Now, they have numerous integrations (including some major ones with companies like Salesforce), and a backlog of companies who want to work with them.

Having a strong company blog can positively impact at least eight other traction channels—SEO, publicity, email marketing, targeting blogs, community building, offline events, existing platforms, and business development.

When it works, it drives in customers like magic. Rick put it like this:

[Our blog] drives search. It drives word of mouth. The blog is top of the funnel. People find the blog, and it's attached to our Web site. We don't market the blog, per se, but we're constantly— several times a week—releasing content that gets shared and drives people to the blog.

TARGETS

- **If you blog, dedicate at least six months to it.** A company blog can take a significant amount of time to start taking off.
- **Do things that don't scale early on.** Reaching out to individuals to share posts, for instance, is okay, because you're building toward a point where your content will spread on its own. Contacting influential industry leaders (on Twitter, etc.), doing guest posts, writing about recent news events,

and creating shareable infographics are all great ways to increase the rate of growth of your audience.

- **Produce in-depth posts you can't find anywhere else.** You need to create quality content to succeed in this traction channel. There is no silver bullet, but a decent approach is to write about problems your target customers have. Another approach (not mutually exclusive) is to run experiments or use data from your company that leads to a surprising conclusion.

CHAPTER FOURTEEN
Email Marketing

If you're like us, you have multiple promotions sitting in your inbox right now—coupons, referrals, sales pitches, and more. This is email marketing. Many companies (Groupon, JackThreads, Thrillist, Zappos) use email marketing as their core traction channel.

Email marketing is a personal channel. Messages from your company sit next to email updates from friends and family. As such, email marketing works best when it is personalized. Email can be tailored to individual customer actions such that every email communication is relevant.

For this channel, we interviewed Colin Nederkoorn, the founder and CEO of Customer.io, a startup that makes it easy for companies to send email based on actions their customers take. Colin explained:

> *If you're running a real business, [email] is still the most effective way to universally reach people who have expressed*

interest in your product or site. For that, it really can't be beat.

Email marketing can be used for all stages of the customer life cycle: building familiarity with prospects, acquiring customers, and retaining the customers you already have.

EMAIL MARKETING FOR FINDING CUSTOMERS

Before we dive in, let us give you a warning. Some companies will buy email lists to send bulk, unsolicited email. That is the very definition of spam. Spam makes recipients angry, hurts future email deliverability efforts, and harms your company in the long run. We do not recommend it.

Luckily, there are many legitimate ways to acquire customers using email. We urge you to build an email list of prospective customers through your other marketing efforts. This is useful whether you end up focusing on this channel or not because a list of interested prospects is an asset that you can draw on for years.

Traction channels such as SEO or content marketing can help you build your email lists. At the bottom of your blog posts and landing pages, simply ask for an email address. Many companies require an email address for people to access premium content, such as videos or white papers. In our interview with Rick Perreault of Unbounce, he stated that this tactic was the single biggest driver of its email list growth.

Another popular approach to building an email list is creating a short, free course related to your area of expertise. These mini-courses are meant to educate potential customers about your problem space and product. At the end of the course you put a call to action, such as asking people to purchase your product, start a free trial, or share something with their friends.

In addition to your own email list, consider advertising on email news-letters complementary to your product. Many email newsletters accept advertisers, and if not, you can contact them directly and ask for a special arrangement.

EMAIL MARKETING FOR ENGAGING CUSTOMERS

Customer activation is a critical and often-overlooked component of building a successful product. "Activating" a customer means getting them to engage with your product enough that they are an active customer. For Twitter, it specifically means sending out a tweet or following five people. For Dropbox, it means successfully installing the application and uploading at least one file.

As you would expect, improving your activation rates can have a significant effect on your business. After all, if a customer never gets the value of your product, how can you expect them to pay for it, or recommend it to others?

Email marketing is a great way to improve your customer activation rates. A popular approach is to create a sequence of emails that slowly exposes your new customers to the key features in your product. Instead of throwing everything at them right away, you can email them five days after they've signed up and say, "Hey, did you know we have this feature?" As Colin explains:

> [Y]ou create the ideal experience for your users when they sign up for your trial. You then create all of the paths they can go down when they fail to go through the ideal experience. And you have emails in place to catch them and help them get back on that [ideal] path.

Let's take Dropbox as an example. If you create an account but never upload a file, you are not active. Maybe you signed up for the site but got busy and forgot about it. When this happens, Dropbox automatically emails you, reminding you to upload a file. With these targeted emails, Dropbox has increased the chance that you will return to the product and become an active user.

For these emails, you should determine the steps *absolutely necessary* to get value from your product. Then create targeted emails to make sure people complete those steps. For those who fail to complete step one, create a message that automatically emails them when they've dropped off. Repeat this at every step where people could quit, and you will see a major uptick in the number of people finishing the activation process.

With tools like Vero and Customer.io, automating these messages is easy. For example, you can use these tools to send an email to people who have not activated their account within three days of signing up for a free trial.

You can also use initial emails to get customer feedback. Colin sends each new Customer.io signup an automated, personal email thirty minutes after they sign up. Here's the email:

Subject: *Help getting started?*

Hey {{ customer.first_name }},
     I'm Colin, CEO of Customer.io. I wanted to reach out to see if you need any help getting started.

Cheers,
Colin

He mentioned that the email receives about a 17 percent reply rate, which is fantastic as far as automated emails go. It opens the channel of communication between Colin and his customers. Through these replies he's learned a great deal about what wasn't working in the product, which has led to many improvements.

EMAIL MARKETING FOR RETAINING CUSTOMERS

For many businesses, email marketing is the most effective channel to bring people back to their sites. Take Twitter as an example. If you're an active Twitter user, think of every email you've ever gotten from them about someone mentioning you in a tweet, a friend of yours who just signed up, or their weekly digest of popular tweets you may have missed. Each one of those emails is meant to keep you active on Twitter.

Your retention emails will depend on the type of product you have. For example, if you have a social networking product, you could send a simple email to customers who haven't signed in for two weeks. Dating services often showcase profiles or mention unread messages. More business-oriented products usually focus on reminders, reports, and information about how you've been using and getting value from the product.

For infrequently used products, email marketing can be the primary form of customer engagement. Mint sends you a weekly financial summary that shows your expenses and income over the previous week. This keeps its product at the forefront of customers' minds and allows it to provide value even if they aren't always signed in. BillGuard, a service that monitors your credit cards for suspicious transactions, sends you a similar report every month.

Email marketing is also one of the best channels to surprise and delight your customers. Brennan Dunn of Planscope (a project planning tool for freelancers) sends a weekly email to his customers telling them how much they made that week. Who wouldn't want to get an email like that? Any sort of communication telling your customers how well they're doing is likely to go over well. Patrick McKenzie, whom we interviewed for SEO, calls this the "you are so awesome" email.

Some companies send emails that showcase your previous engagement with the product. For example, photo sites will send you pictures you took a year ago. These emails achieve both goals: they often make you feel good on an emotional level, and also invite you to come back and upload more pictures.

EMAIL MARKETING FOR REVENUE

Groupon and many other companies use email to generate hundreds of millions of dollars in revenue. Patrick said his email subscribers were seventy times more likely to buy one of his courses than those from other traction channels (targeting blogs, SEO, and content marketing).

A common way to drive revenue through email marketing is sending a series of emails aimed at upselling customers. As an example, WP Engine, a WordPress hosting company, uses such a campaign to get customers on one of their premium plans. They've built a WordPress blog speed tester tool (at speed.wpengine.com) where interested prospects can enter their site URL and email address to get a free report about their site's performance.

Over the course of a month, WP Engine will then send that prospect an email course about WordPress speed and scalability—three quick ways to improve your site speed, why hosting is important for business, etc. Near the end of this mini-course, WP Engine will make a pitch to sign up for its premium WordPress hosting service.

This seven-email sequence leads to a better conversion rate than driving potential people to a sales landing page. In fact, many companies like WP Engine now use advertising to drive leads to a landing page where they ask for an email rather than a sale. They then will use email marketing to sell a prospect over the course of a month or so.

When WP Engine has prospects they know are not ready to convert, they put them on a different list where they send them less frequent (monthly) emails with relevant content. When it later comes time for these prospects to go looking for premium WordPress hosting, you can guess where they go.

Email retargeting is another tool you can use for revenue. For example, if one of your customers abandoned a shopping cart, send her a targeted email a day or two later with a special offer for whatever item she left in the cart. Targeted emails will always convert better than an email asking for a sale out of the blue.

For feature-based freemium products, emails that explain a premium feature a customer is missing out on can have high conversion rates. For example, if you run a dating Web site, you can explain that upgrading to a premium plan will lead to more dates. If you have a subscription product, ask them to upgrade to annual billing, which guarantees they will not cancel within the next year.

Similarly, if you run a scaled pricing business (e.g., you pay $9/month for five users, $20/month for ten users, and so on), you can set up special emails for customers nearing their plan limits and ask them to upgrade. When you're about to run out of Skype credits, Skype will email you asking you to re-up or upgrade to a subscription service.

EMAIL MARKETING FOR REFERRALS

Due to the personal nature of email, it is also excellent for generating customer referrals. If a friend emails you to tell you about a new product she is enjoying, you're far more likely to try it than if you saw her mention it briefly on Facebook.

Groupon generates referrals by giving people an incentive to tell their friends about discounts. Unless a certain number of people have purchased a Groupon, the discount is not valid. Thus, as someone who wants 50 percent off their meal at Cheesecake Factory, we will happily email our friends so the deal happens.

This kind of referral program was a major growth driver for Dropbox as well. In order to get more free space, users send referral emails asking their friends to check out Dropbox. If a friend signs up, both people get extra free space. This referral program built on top of email has been Dropbox's biggest growth mechanism and has led to tens of millions of users.

Some consumer apps, and even some B2B companies like Asana, will ask their customers to import their address books to share the site with their friends. This marketing tactic touches elements of both viral and email marketing and can be extremely effective. In fact, many of the viral products you know of (Hotmail, Facebook, LinkedIn) grew by cleverly using email marketing.

EMAIL MARKETING TACTICS

Deliverability is a key factor in email. For many technical reasons, your email messages may not be reaching their intended recipients. Most companies use an email-marketing provider like MailChimp or Constant Contact to send their emails. These companies help ensure deliverability.

As with other traction channels, testing is essential to maximize this channel's impact. Effective email campaigns A/B test every aspect: subjects, formats, images, timing, and more. Timing is especially relevant to get higher open rates: many marketers suggest sending emails between nine a.m. and twelve p.m. in your customer's time zone or scheduling emails to reach them at the time they registered for your email list (e.g., for people who signed up for your list at eight p.m., email them at eight p.m.).

One of email's strengths is that it's a way to get feedback from your customers. One trick Colin told us about was not to send any email that comes from a "Noreply" email address (e.g., noreply@facebook.com). Intead, use that opportunity to send the automated email from a personal address and allow the recipient to reply with questions or problems they have. This can be great for support, for feature requests, and for upselling existing customers.

Last, an effective email sequence will be meaningless if you don't have great email copy. Copywriting is an art on its own, but we suggest checking out some of the resources and information that Copy Hackers provides. An email campaign can easily go from a waste of time to wildly profitable just by tweaking a few words and headlines.

TARGETS

- **Personalize your email marketing messages.** Email marketing is a personal traction channel. Messages come into your inbox along with email from your friends and family.
- **Build an email list of prospective customers whether you end up focusing on this traction channel or not.** You can utilize email marketing at any step of your relationship with a customer, including customer acquisition, activation, retention, and revenue generation.
- **Set up a series of automated emails.** Often called life cycle or drip sequences, this technique works best when the series

of emails adapts to how people have interacted with your product.

- **Use online tools to test and optimize email campaigns.** These tools have built-in templates and A/B testing ability and will track open and click rates.

CHAPTER FIFTEEN
Viral Marketing

Viral marketing is the process of getting your existing customers to refer others to your product. You've seen examples of this traction channel in action any time a friend's Pinterest post appeared in your Facebook feed, or whenever you've received an automated email from a friend telling you about a product.

In the context of startups, literally "going viral" means that every user you acquire brings in *at least one other user.* That new user then invites at least one other user, and so on. This creates true exponential growth. Though difficult to sustain, it's been the driving force behind the explosive growth of consumer startups like Facebook, Twitter, and WhatsApp.

As great as your product may be, true viral growth is unlikely. However, this channel is so powerful that even if you can't achieve exponential growth, you can often still get meaningful growth through viral marketing. When viral loops are working, customers sign up in great numbers at very low acquisition cost.

Think about the numbers. Suppose that when your customers sign up, you get each of them to refer one new customer within the first week. You'll go from ten customers to twenty that first week, and keep doubling every week thereafter without any additional marketing! That's true viral growth.

If only every other customer refers a friend—a result that's really pretty good—it will take forever to get from ten to twenty on its own. But still, even in this case, viral marketing is helping you get two customers for every one you bring in. We will walk through this viral math in detail in this chapter.

We interviewed Andrew Chen, founder of Muzy (an app with more than 25 million users) and one of the experts in the viral marketing world. According to Andrew, this traction channel is becoming increasingly important as Facebook, email, and app stores have emerged as "super-platforms" with billions of active users each. As a result, companies can go viral faster than ever before. Dropbox, Instagram, Snapchat, and Pinterest are great examples: they all leveraged virality through these super-platforms to acquire tens of millions of users in just a few years.

VIRAL MARKETING STRATEGY

Viral marketing strategy begins and ends with viral loops. A viral loop in its most basic form is a three-step process:

1. A customer is exposed to your product or service.
2. That customers tells a set of potential customers about your product or service.
3. These potential customers are exposed to your product or service, and some portion become customers themselves.

The process then begins again with this new set of customers. It's called a loop because it repeats over and over again: as your customers refer other customers, those customers refer others, and so on.

Though viral loops share the same basic structure, each company executes them differently. Dropbox's loop is different from Pinterest's, which is different from Skype's. We're going to describe the main kinds of viral loops and show you how companies have used them to succeed.

The oldest form of virality occurs when your product is so remarkable that people naturally tell others about it—pure word of mouth. Word of mouth drove Facebook's early growth among college students, before they started building in more explicit viral hooks (email invites, adding your friends via address books, etc.). Word of mouth also causes many movies, books, diets, and TV shows to take off.

Inherent virality occurs when you can get value from a product only by inviting other customers. For example, if your friends don't have Skype, the application is worthless. Apps like Snapchat and WhatsApp also fall into this category. This type of virality comes with the advantage of "network effects," where the value of the network increases as more people get on it. That is, the more people who are on Skype, the more valuable it becomes.

Other products grow by encouraging collaboration. In this case, the product is still valuable on its own, but becomes more so as you invite others. Google Docs is useful alone, but it is far more valuable when used collaboratively. This type of viral loop can take longer to spread if your customers don't need to immediately collaborate. However, once they do, strong network effects kick in as the service becomes a central tool around which collaboration occurs.

Another common case is to embed virality into communications from the product. Hotmail put "Get a free email account with Hotmail. Sign up now" as a default signature, and Apple similarly appends "Sent from my iPhone." As a result, every message sent spreads the word about the product. Many software products do this with their free customers. MailChimp, Weebly, UserVoice, and Desk.com all add branding to free customers' emails and Web sites by default, which can be removed by becoming a paying user.

Products can also incentivize their customers to move through their viral loops and tell others about the product. Dropbox gives you more space if you get friends to sign up. Airbnb, Uber, PayPal, and Gilt give you account credits for referring the product to friends.

Companies like reddit and YouTube have grown virally by using embedded buttons and widgets. On each video page, YouTube provides the code snippet necessary to embed a video on any Web site. You've probably also noticed such buttons for Facebook and Twitter on many Web pages: each button encourages sharing, which exposes the product to more and more people.

Another type of viral loop leverages social networks to attract new customers to a product or service. In this case, a user's activities are broadcast to his social connections, often more than once. If you've spent any time on Facebook, we're sure you've seen your friends liking articles on other sites, playing songs on Spotify, or pinning content on Pinterest.

It is instructive to think about how each of these types could possibly apply to your product or service. You can combine them as well. In fact, when you can get multiple forms working together, your viral loops will be that much stronger.

Take Uber for example. Riding in a cab is often something you do with another person, meaning every new usage could demonstrate the product to a potential new customer. This is a form of inherent virality because people naturally find themselves together when taking an Uber. It also has parts of collaborative and incentivized virality because it is often useful to take an Uber together, both logistically and financially.

To fully appreciate the viral loop concept and to understand whether viral marketing can work for you, you have to do a tiny bit of math. This viral math helps you quickly identify how close you are to getting traction through viral marketing, as well as which areas you need to focus on. The two key factors that drive viral growth are the viral coefficient and the viral cycle time.

The viral coefficient, or K, is the number of additional customers you can get for each customer you bring in.

The viral coefficient formula is:

$$K = i * \text{conversion percentage}$$

where K is the viral coefficient, i is the number of invites sent per user, and conversion percentage is the percentage of customers who sign up after receiving an invitation. For example, if your customers send out an average of three invites and two of those people usually convert to new customers, your viral coefficient would be:

$$K = 3 * (2/3) = 2$$

If you were to add one hundred new customers in a week, you could expect them to send out three hundred more invites to your site and two hundred more customers to sign on with you as a result. That's viral growth!

Any viral coefficient above 1 will result in exponential growth, meaning that each new user brings in more than one additional user, creating true exponential growth. Any viral coefficient over 0.5 helps your efforts to grow considerably.

There are two variables that affect your viral coefficient. The first is the number of invites (i) that each user sends out. If you can increase the average number of invites that each user sends out, say from one invite per user to two, you will double your viral coefficient. To push this number up as high as you can, consider including features that encourage sharing, such as posting to social networks.

The second variable is the conversion percentage. If your product is being shared but not generating new customers, you won't go viral. As with invites, if you double your conversion percentage (by doing things like testing different signup flows), you double your viral coefficient. The best signup flows reduce friction by making things simpler, such as cutting out pages or signup fields. For example, the conversion steps for a standard Web application often involve clicking on a link and filling out a form to create an account. In that case, you could break the conversion percentage into two percentages.

$$K = i * \text{conversion percentage} = i * \text{click-through percentage} * \text{signup percentage}$$

When you break out conversion percentage in this way, you can determine the weakest part of your equation and focus on it. Your click-through percentage may be great, but your signup percentage may be subpar. This makes it clear what to focus on—the area where you can make the biggest positive impact.

Viral cycle time is a measure of how long it takes a user to go through your viral loop. For example, if it takes an average of three days for invites to convert into customers, your viral cycle time is three days.

Two viral loops with the same viral coefficient but different viral cycle times will end up with dramatically different outcomes: the shorter this time, the better. Viral cycle time explains the explosive growth of a company like YouTube, whose cycle times can occur in a matter of minutes—someone sees a video, clicks on it to go to the site, then copies the link and sends it to friends.

Shortening your viral cycle time drastically increases the rate at which you go viral, and is one of the first things you should focus on improving if using this channel. To shorten it, create urgency or incentivize customers to move through your viral loops. Additionally, make every step in your funnel *as simple as possible* to increase the number of people who complete it. That's why YouTube provides embed codes for each video: to make it simple for any user to add videos to her site or blog.

VIRAL MARKETING TACTICS

To pursue this traction channel effectively, you need to measure your viral coefficient and viral cycle time from the start. Consider those measurements your baseline. Then you need to get your viral coefficient up and viral cycle time down to levels that yield enough new customers to produce steady growth for your business.

We suggest running as many A/B tests as you can. Best practice suggests focusing for weeks at a time on one major area (say your signup conversion rate), trying everything you can think of to improve that metric, and then moving on to another metric that needs improvement as you run out of ideas. Andrew notes that this process can take time:

> *Even expert teams will take one or two engineers working*
> *two to three months, minimum, to implement and optimize*

a new viral channel to the point where it's growing quickly without any ad spend. Once it gets going, though, it becomes easier to incrementally improve and grow the product. You need a strong strategy, and need to spend considerable time and resources to get something going.

As you come up with your initial strategy for viral loops, create a simple dashboard of what needs to go up to be viral. Understand how new users end up helping you acquire more new users and do a lot of A/B tests (several per week) to try and improve the metrics.

The best way to approach this testing is to map out every aspect of your viral loop. How many steps are in the loop? What are all the ways people can enter into the loop (landing pages, ads, invites)?

Literally draw a map of the entire process and try cutting out unnecessary steps (extra signup pages, unnecessary forms or fields to fill out, etc.) and increase areas or mechanisms where customers can send out invitations. Doing so will improve your viral equation by increasing your invites sent and your conversion percentage.

We interviewed Ashish Kundra, founder of Indian dating network myZamana, about the effectiveness of sharing mechanisms. He said that there are numerous viral mechanics you can build into your product, but to be really successful people need to like and repeatedly use the product.

To drive usage, myZamana sends targeted emails to users based on actions they take on the site. As people use the site, their actions generate invitations to other users (e.g., "Mark liked you!"). The more people use the product, the more notifications are sent out.

A nonuser's first exposure to a product often occurs when a current user sends an invitation. The nonuser will then have to decide what to do with the invitation or whether it's worth her time to even open it. Your goal in designing these invitations is to get potential customers to engage with the invite and follow the link (or take the next step) that the invitation contains.

Invitations that work best are short and succinct. Sign up for the most viral services you can think of and you'll see what we mean. Additionally, personal hooks really help.

People are overloaded with information about services they don't use. This makes many people hesitant to sign up for a product they have not experienced themselves. However, viral growth is impossible if you have a low signup percentage because then you have no chance of a decent viral coefficient.

For this reason, some companies allow people to use portions of their product without signing up. This allows potential customers to test-drive the product without making any sort of commitment.

The pages that prospective customers land on from invitations are called conversion pages. Conversion pages work best when they use the same messaging as the invitations that preceded them. For example, if in the invitation you say so-and-so referred you to this product, you can put the exact same message on the conversion page.

Understanding exactly why people are clicking on your links and signing up (e.g., curiosity, obligation, etc.) will help you think of better ways to improve your viral loop. Surveys, sites like UserTesting.com, and asking people directly are great ways to uncover this psychology.

Here are some of the more common items to test and optimize:

- Button vs. text links
- Location of your call to actions
- Size, color, and contrast of your action buttons
- Page speed
- Adding images
- Headlines
- Site copy
- Testimonials
- Signs of social proof (such as pictures of happy customers, case studies, press mentions, and statistics about product usage)
- Number of form fields
- Allowing users to test the product before signing up

- Ease of signup (Facebook Connect, Twitter login, etc.)
- Length of the signup process (the shorter you can make the process, the higher your conversion percentage will be)

First focus on changes that, if they worked, would result in a 5–10x improvement in a key metric. This could be something like an entirely new email auto-responder sequence, a new Web site design, or a new onboarding flow. Once you've made big changes, then optimize the smaller stuff.

Almost no optimization is too small to test: even changing one word in a headline can have a significant impact. Because viral growth compounds, a 1 percent improvement can make a big difference over the long term.

With all viral (or near-viral) growth, there will be subgroups of customers growing far more rapidly than your total customer base. We call these subgroups "viral pockets." Figure out if you have viral pockets by calculating your viral coefficient on distinct subsets of your customers, such as those from a particular country, age group, or other trait.

For example, you may be taking off in Indonesia while not doing as well in Australia. Once you find a viral pocket, you may want to cater to this group by optimizing text in their native language or some other way that will improve their experience.

Since most viral loops are not self-sustaining, you need a constant stream of new customers entering your viral loop. This process is called "seeding." When seeding new customers for your viral loop, you're looking for people in your target audience who have not been exposed to your product. SEO and online ads are good, inexpensive candidates for seeding.

CONCLUSION

Because of the potential to acquire free customers, many startups try to go viral. Andrew mentioned that he sees companies making the same mistakes:

- Products that aren't inherently viral trying to add a bunch of viral features
- Bad products that aren't adding value trying to go viral

- Not doing enough A/B tests to really find improvements (assume one to three out of every ten will yield positive results)
- Not understanding how users are currently communicating/ sharing, and bolting on "best practice" strategies (Just add Facebook "like" buttons!)
- Not getting coaching/guidance from people who've already done it
- Thinking about virality as a tactic rather than a deep part of a product strategy

As he told us, the best way to figure out the right kind of loop to build is simple: copy those who have done it before.

> *The easiest way, for a beginner—copy someone else's viral loop until yours starts to work in a similar way. Copying someone else's loop down to the detail is important, including text copy, etc. These are the things that drive performance.*
>
> *Make it something that the user wants to do, because it creates value from them. Skype with no contacts is useless—so by helping people import their address books and invite people, you're doing them a service.*

Even if you cannot truly go viral, you can still use this channel to spur rapid growth by compounding your efforts on other traction channels. If you are getting a steady stream of new customers through other channels, build a viral loop to bring in more and more customers.

TARGETS

- **Build a viral loop into the product.** There are several types of viral loops, including word of mouth, inherent, collaborative, communicative, incentives, embedded, and social. Startups can combine and change types over time, but generally these loops need to be built into the product to work successfully.

- **Shorten viral cycle time.** The shorter this time, the more loops will occur and the faster you will grow.
- **Look for viral pockets.** You might already be viral in a subgroup of your customers. Find that subgroup and focus on it.
- **More than in any other channel, test, test, test.** Successful viral strategy involves constant testing, measurement, and trying new things. It is a numbers and creativity game. No test is too small, as small changes can have big effects over time. Viral loops that work well often have extremely simple components (forms, copy, email, etc.).

CHAPTER SIXTEEN
Engineering as Marketing

Your team's engineering skills can get your startup traction directly by building tools and resources that reach more people. We call this traction channel "engineering as marketing." You make useful tools like calculators, widgets, and educational microsites to get your company in front of potential customers.

These tools generate leads and expand your customer base. In this chapter we present examples of companies like HubSpot and RJMetrics that have successfully used this underutilized channel for rapid growth.

ENGINEERING AS MARKETING STRATEGY

HubSpot, a marketing automation software company, has reached tens of millions in revenue in a few short years. One key to its success is a free marketing review tool the company created called Marketing Grader.

When you enter your site's Web address into Marketing Grader, you get back a customized report about how well you're doing with your online marketing (social media mentions, blog post shares, basic SEO). This tool is free and gives you valuable information. It also provides HubSpot with information they use to qualify you as a potential prospect. After all, someone who wants to evaluate the success of their site's marketing is a good candidate for HubSpot's main product. These are quality leads.

We spoke with HubSpot's founder, Dharmesh Shah, about Marketing Grader. His story provides insight on where ideas for engineering as marketing tools come from:

> *The early story of [Marketing] Grader is interesting. There were only three people at HubSpot at the time. My cofounder and I would regularly "sell" (in the early days, a lot of those sales calls were with friends, and friends of friends). One of the initial steps in the sales process was for me to get a sense for how good a given company's Web site was at inbound marketing. My cofounder [Brian Halligan] would constantly send me Web sites he wanted me to take a look at so we could determine if they were a good fit.*
>
> *After a few days of this, I got tired of going through the manual steps (look at Alexa, look at their page titles, check out their domain, etc.). So I built an application to automate that process for me. On a related note, I had also started angel investing at the time, and I used the same process to assess the marketing savviness of potential startups I was considering investing in. Once the app was built (it didn't take more than a few days for the initial version), I thought it might be useful for other people, so I registered "websitegrader.com" and made the app available publicly. We eventually started collecting email addresses in the app, and kept iterating on it.*

Since HubSpot launched Marketing Grader, more than 3 million sites have used it. Dharmesh said that it accounts for a large portion of the fifty thousand–plus leads HubSpot gets each month.

Marketing Grader is so powerful for HubSpot because it precisely serves the needs of its target audience. It's a low-friction way to draw leads into the HubSpot sales funnel. Engineering as marketing is particularly effective for HubSpot because Marketing Grader complements its primary product so well.

Another company that nails engineering as marketing is Moz, the leader in SEO software. Two of its free SEO tools, Followerwonk and Open Site Explorer, have driven tens of thousands of leads for Moz. Like Marketing Grader, each solves a problem that an ideal Moz customer has. Followerwonk allows people to analyze their Twitter followers and get tips on growing their audience. Open Site Explorer allows people to see where sites are getting links, which is valuable competitive intelligence for any SEO campaign.

A key feature of these tools is their ease of use: prospects simply go to the site and enter a domain name or Twitter handle. Once someone uses the tools, companies can begin to engage these potential customers through other traction channels like sales and email marketing.

WP Engine, a WordPress hosting provider, is another prime example of a company using this channel successfully. The hosting market is saturated with hundreds of hosting companies, yet WP Engine has cornered the market on high-end WordPress hosting. This is thanks in part to its free tool that checks how fast your WordPress site loads.

The WP Engine speed testing tool asks for only an email address in exchange for a detailed report about your site's speed. It also gives you the option to opt in for a free mini-course about improving the speed of your blog. Once WP Engine has a user's email, it sends her tips about improving her site speed and ends with a sales pitch.

Dharmesh mentioned that it helps him to think of these tools as marketing *assets* with ongoing returns, rather than ads that result in a one-time boost.

> *I think of free tools as content (albeit interactive content). At HubSpot, we really believe in marketing channels that have high leverage (i.e., write it or build it once—and get value forever). As such, we take a very geeky and analytical approach*

to marketing. We think of each piece of content (blog article, app, video, whatever) as a marketing asset. This asset creates a return—often indefinitely.

We contrast that to buying an ad, which does not scale as well. When you advertise, the money you're spending is what drives how much attention you get. Want more clicks? Spend more money. Contrast this to inbound marketing whereby the cost of producing a piece of content is relatively constant. But, if it generates 10x more leads in a month, your marginal cost for those extra leads is almost zero. Further, with advertising (outbound marketing), the traffic you get generally stops when you stop paying. With inbound marketing, even after *you stop producing new content, the old content can still drive ongoing visitors and leads.*

The case for spending engineering resources on marketing becomes much stronger when you think about the resulting tools as assets. These tools have the potential to become a continual source of leads that make up the majority of your traction.

ENGINEERING AS MARKETING TACTICS

One way to boost your efforts in this traction channel is to take advantage of cyclical behavior. Take Codecademy's Code Year microsite, which launched at the beginning of 2012. Many people claim to want to learn how to code, but don't follow through. Code Year addressed that issue by asking people to enter their email address to receive a free lesson about programming each week during 2012. More than 450,000 individuals signed up on CodeYear.com, nearly doubling Codecademy's user base at the time.

Similarly, Patrick McKenzie from Bingo Card Creator makes holiday-themed microsites for Halloween, Christmas, and other holidays. Since they are tied to the holidays, Bingo Card Creator can use them year after year. In Codecademy's case, you could actually sign up for Code Year at any point during the year and still receive a lesson each week.

When Gabriel wrote blog posts about search privacy, he got a big response from readers. After he engaged with commenters in social media channels it became clear that this is a topic that really resonated with people. Gabriel had the idea that a microsite might address people's concerns more fully while simultaneously exposing his search engine, DuckDuckGo, to a broader audience.

In 2011, Gabriel built such a microsite, DontTrack.us, which showed how Google tracks your searches and why that can harm you. The site raised awareness about these practices and spread virally. At the same time, readers learned that DuckDuckGo does not track people or store their personal information.

Even after the initial wave of press and users, this microsite has been useful. As unpredictable events unfold (like news of NSA tracking) or predictable events reoccur (like Data Privacy Day), the traffic on the ever-present microsite persists. Users of DuckDuckGo often send the site to friends and family to explain the issues surrounding search tracking. The strategy worked so well that DuckDuckGo now has several microsites.

To really maximize impact, put your microsites and tools on their own domains. This simple technique does two things. First, it makes them much easier to share. Second, you can do well with SEO by picking a name that people search often so your tool is more naturally discoverable.

Chris Fralic, former head of business development at Delicious and Half.com, told us that creating a Delicious bookmark widget more than tripled the adoption of its social bookmarking product.

How many times have you seen Facebook, Twitter, and other sharing buttons on a site? For each of those widgets (e.g., Facebook, Stumble-Upon, Google+, and Twitter buttons), a company used engineering resources to create a marketing tool that was embeddable on sites. These widgets drive engagement, traffic, and traction for these social platforms and the sites that use these tools.

CASE STUDY: RJMETRICS

We spoke with Robert Moore, founder of RJMetrics (an e-commerce analytics company) to learn how they've used this traction channel to drive the majority of their leads and sales. As an engineer himself, Robert said he's been using his engineering skills to bring in customers since he founded the company.

For example, RJMetrics uses its own product to discover interesting trends on some of the most popular social media sites like Twitter, Tumblr, Instagram, and Pinterest. For example, one popular post was entitled "*BuzzFeed* Posts: What's the Magic Number for 'Best Of' Lists?"

These posts produced big traffic spikes when they launched, and led to a lot of long-tail opportunities as people discovered the content over time. Robert mentioned that they've been approached multiple times by writers for major publications who want to cite them as a source. OkCupid has a similar strategy that we covered under content marketing.

Though its engineering efforts have certainly helped its content marketing, RJMetrics seriously began to use this channel when it started building tools and microsites. It owns and creates content for domains like cohortanalysis.com and querymongo.com, which contain keywords a potential RJMetrics customer would search for.

In the case of querymongo.com, RJMetrics built a tool that translates SQL queries to MongoDB syntax (two database technologies). This is useful for developers or product managers starting to use MongoDB but who are still more familiar with SQL. It also drives leads for RJMetrics, because anyone doing data analysis is a potential customer for its main product. Querymongo is RJ's highest-trafficked microsite and drives hundreds of leads per month.

Robert said they look for high ROI on engineering time: if a few days of engineering time can drive hundreds of leads, that's an investment they make whenever they can.

CONCLUSION

Engineering as marketing creates lasting assets that can serve as the engine for your growth. Zack Linford, the founder of Optimozo and Conversion Voodoo, talked about how building tools can help with publicity and SEO, while also nailing down the core value proposition for your product. As he mentioned in our interview:

> *Building noteworthy tools that your target audience finds useful is a solid way to gain traction that also pays dividends down the road by helping build your SEO. A simple roadmap to executing this technical strategy includes:*
>
> - *Providing something of true value for free, with no strings attached.*
> - *Making that offering extremely relevant to your core business.*
> - *Demonstrating that value as quickly as possible.*

When you build valuable tools for prospective customers, you get more leads, a stronger brand, and increased awareness while also solving a problem for the individuals you want to target.

Dharmesh mentioned that engineering as marketing is especially valuable because so few companies use it:

> *I'm a big believer in using an engineering approach to marketing. But I'm biased (being an engineer myself). And yes, there are many other marketing channels available, but creating applications has a unique investment/return profile. Since it is considerably harder to build a very popular application, fewer people do it: so the "free apps" channel is usually less saturated.*
>
> *The best companies to use this apps-powered model are software companies. In this case, they can launch complementary apps—or subsets—for free. This not only creates value that draws people in, it also educates people on what the main product does.*

Companies have a hard time using engineering resources for anything but product development. Any technical focus on something other than product seems wasted since engineering time is so expensive. As a result, most founders and product managers use all their engineering resources to build new features for a product or service that's struggling to acquire customers. Don't make the same mistake. Instead, consider using some of that engineering time to build a tool that moves the needle for your business.

TARGETS

- **Create a stand-alone, low-friction site to engage potential customers.** Make sure it naturally leads to your main offering. The case for spending engineering resources on marketing becomes much stronger when you think about these marketing tools as long-term assets that bring in new leads indefinitely after only a small amount of up-front investment.
- **Look internally for site and tool ideas.** Perhaps you have already started creating something for yourself that could also be used by potential customers? Another approach is to turn a popular blog post into a microsite.
- **Make them as simple as possible.** Single-purpose tools that solve obvious pain points are best. Put them on their own Web sites and make them easy to find, particularly through search engines.

CHAPTER SEVENTEEN
Business Development (BD)

Business development is like sales with one key distinction: it is primarily focused on exchanging value through partnerships, whereas sales primarily focuses on exchanging dollars for a product. With sales, you're selling directly to a customer. With business development, you're partnering to reach customers in a way that benefits both parties.

We interviewed Chris Fralic, former senior business development executive at AOL, Half.com, eBay, and Delicious, and current partner at First Round Capital. Chris described how he used business development successfully at each of his startups (all of which were acquired).

Many companies get traction through business development. Even Google, a company whose early success is often attributed only to a superior product, got most of its initial traction from two key partnerships. In 1999, it partnered with Netscape to be the default search engine for the popular Netscape Navigator Web browser. Google also reached an agreement with Yahoo!, then (and still) one of the largest Web properties in existence, to power its online searches. These two deals were critical to Google's eventual success as the world's largest search engine.

BUSINESS DEVELOPMENT STRATEGY

Here are the major types of business development partnerships:

Standard partnerships—In a standard partnership, two companies work together to make one or both of their products better by leveraging the unique capabilities of the other. One prominent example is the Apple/Nike partnership that resulted in the Nike+ shoe that communicates with your iPod or iPhone to track your runs and play music.

Joint ventures—In a joint venture, two companies work together to create an entirely new product offering. These types of deals are complex and often require large investments, long periods of time, and (sometimes) equity exchanges. If you've ever bought a bottled Starbucks Frappuccino or Doubleshot Espresso, you've purchased a product that's the result of the decade-long joint venture between Starbucks and Pepsi.

Licensing—Licensing works well when one company has a strong brand that an upstart wants to use in a new product or service. To use another Starbucks example, the company lent its brand to an ice cream manufacturer that wanted to create Starbucks-flavored ice cream. Other startups, such as Spotify and Grooveshark, are forced into licensing agreements by the nature of their business. They can't use music content without first licensing it from the record labels that own it.

Distribution deals—In these deals, one party provides a product or service to the other in return for access to potential customers. Groupon's core business is structured like this: it works with a restaurant or store to offer a discount to Groupon's mailing list. Paul English, founder of Kayak, told us how a distribution deal with AOL was responsible for Kayak's early traction.

Through this partnership, Kayak used its search technology to power an AOL-owned travel search engine, which drove a lot of traffic right out of the gate.

Supply partnerships—These types of partnerships help you secure key inputs, which are essential for certain products. As we'll see, Half.com formed several to ensure that it had enough books to sell when it launched its online bookstore. Other supply partnerships include Hulu's relationship with channel partners and deals between suppliers and companies like Walmart.

Business development can drive some amazing outcomes for your startup. However, getting traction from this channel requires something that few companies do well: strategic thinking.

For business development to work well, you must have a clear understanding of your company objectives. What metrics do you need to hit in order to maximize your chances of success? How can partnerships help you get there? Good BD deals align with your company and product strategy and are focused on critical product and distribution milestones. These deals should help you hit your key metrics, whether growth, revenue, or product related. If you're following Bullseye and Critical Path, you should have already defined your traction goal and the milestones you need to hit to reach it.

This sounds simple and obvious, but in practice it is difficult. If a big company says it'll work with you, but only in this other way that doesn't strictly align with your traction goal, it is still extremely tempting. So tempting, in fact, that many startups will waste resources on these deals even though they are off their Critical Path. Business development requires discipline.

Chris explained how he approached BD at Half.com:

> In the case of Half.com, there were three key things that we needed before we launched. Number one, the site had to work. We needed technology partners (back in the pre–Amazon Cloud days) to ensure people could actually use the site.
>
> Then there was inventory. We decided we needed one

million books, movies, etc., at launch because that sounded like a nice big number. So my team and I worked on how we get product on the shelves. It was our job (prior to launch) to find inventory and get it listed on the site.

The third was to get distribution. So we went out and created one of the early affiliate programs and did distribution and marketing partnerships.

Once their objectives were identified, Chris and his team were able to form partnerships that allowed them to launch with one of the largest selections of books and movies anywhere at the time.

Understanding a partner's goals is key to creating a mutually beneficial relationship. Chris mentioned that startups are often focused on themselves and their needs without considering why a potential partner should make the deal:

It's research and learning and understanding your partner's business before you start picking up the phone or sending emails. You need to understand what's on their side of the table—what are their issues?

To pick one example, we wanted to find books that were half off and find big quantities of inventory. So I started doing research to find big piles of used inventory and literally started calling people, asking people questions to understand how their business worked. We found out how products moved from book publishers out to the Borders of the world, where it came back to and where it accumulated when it didn't sell. Once we found out where, we ended up getting partnerships with those people. I even flew to Atlanta and literally worked in a used bookstore for a day.

You need to understand *why* a potential partner should want to work with you. What are their incentives? Just as you evaluate potential partnerships in terms of your core metrics, they will be doing the same.

You should also seek out forward-thinking partners. Often that means finding an advocate inside a large company or working with a company that has done deals with startups in the past.

Unfortunately, not every partnership will end up working. Thus, it makes sense to build a pipeline of deals. Charlie O'Donnell, partner at VC firm Brooklyn Bridge Ventures, suggests maintaining a large list of potential partners:

> *Create an exhaustive list of all of your possible [partners]. Don't ever list Condé Nast without listing every single other publisher you can think of. Make a very simple spreadsheet: Company, Partner Type (Publisher, Carrier, Reseller, etc.), Contact Person/Email, Size, Relevance, Ease of Use, and then a subjective priority score. That list should be exhaustive. There's no reason why any company shouldn't have fifty potential business development partners in their pipeline, maybe one hundred, and be actively working the phones, inboxes, and pounding the pavement to get the deals you need to get—be it for distribution, revenue, PR, or just to outflank a competitor. The latter is totally underutilized. If you go in and impress the top fifty folks in your space, it makes it that much harder for a competitor to get a deal done—because you're seen as the category leader.*

Once you have a list of potential partners, send it to your investors, friends, and advisers for warm introductions.

Chris Fralic suggests putting potential partners into buckets based on attributes. For example, you might categorize based on revenue numbers, distribution reach, or inventory capabilities. Then, at the end of this process, choose ten to twenty partners to focus your business development efforts on. As he said:

> *People tend to get caught up on the names—"is this a known name"—and place more emphasis on that than what might*

be more important elements. So I'd encourage people to think about the attributes of your partner. So rather than saying "I want to go after XYZ brand," say "We want to go after Internet retailers that are between 50 and 250 on the IR [Internet Retailer] 500—because that puts them in this kind of revenue range—and have a director of e-commerce."

Chris pitched all kinds of deals during his time at Delicious, the social bookmarking site. While he was there, he worked on deals with *The Washington Post*, Mozilla, and Wikipedia to integrate Delicious tags.

Delicious approached its potential partners with a clear idea of how each of them would benefit from a partnership. For *The Washington Post*, the value proposition was to use Delicious's social bookmarks to optimize content for social media. *The Washington Post*'s decision to partner was made even easier because it was a simple integration with very little downside.

After Delicious integrated with *The Washington Post*, the number of sites interested in a Delicious extension skyrocketed because of the *Post*'s role as a media leader. It even made other partnerships, like the browser integration with Mozilla's Firefox, possible:

The even more transformative partnership we did at Delicious was with Mozilla. [Mozilla] ended up promoting the Delicious extension for the Firefox browser in a really big way when they did an upgrade to Firefox 2.0. The net of it was that when huge portions of their audience were upgrading, one of the first things they saw was the Delicious extension. It ultimately more than tripled our user base, just from that partnership.

Chris stressed that you can be assured that not every deal will close; in fact, most deals won't. For example, Delicious pursued an integration deal with Wikipedia that failed. Delicious was able to get traction from business development because it developed a large pipeline of potential deals.

BUSINESS DEVELOPMENT TACTICS

Once you have a few partners you're targeting, the real action starts. You start approaching potential partners with a value-focused proposition that outlines why they should work with you. Often these are larger companies. Brenda Spoonemore, former senior VP of interactive services at the NBA, put it like this:

> *What do you have that they [big companies] need? You're more focused than they are. You have an idea and you're solving a problem. You've developed content or technology and you have a focus. That is very difficult to do at a big corporation.*

To approach these deals, you want to first identify the right contact at your target company. Some companies will have a business development department that handles partnerships, but—depending on the deal—it could be someone like a product director or C-level executive you want to engage with.

The most important thing is to find out who is in charge of the metric you've targeted. If you think your partnership will help your partner sell more T-shirts, be sure to talk to the person most in charge of selling more T-shirts. If your product will help your partner get more satisfied power users, be sure to talk to the person most charged with pleasing power users. Just because you're offering a Web site widget doesn't mean the Web site team is the ideal set of stakeholders.

Once she is identified, you want to try to get a warm introduction to that person. With each introduction, you should provide the mutual contact with an overview of your proposal that can easily be forwarded. Then be sure to follow up and set time lines for the next steps. Chris Fralic mentioned that it was key for him to get a meeting or phone call set up as quickly as possible—sometimes even on the same day.

After the proposal stage comes negotiation of a term sheet. The key terms will usually be the lifetime of the deal, exclusivity, how payments work (if any), the level of commitment between partners, any guarantees in the deal, and revenue sharing agreements.

Both Chris and Brenda suggest making the negotiation and term sheet as simple as possible—often just one page. The simpler you can make it to work together (and the fewer lawyers who need to get involved), the easier partnering will be.

Keeping it simple is especially good advice for technology partnerships. With engineering time so valuable, do as much as you can to make it easy for potential partners to work with you. For example, Delicious built *The Washington Post* a custom interface for its readers to post bookmarks. Rather than involving the *Post*'s IT resources, Delicious made it easy to get it set up and going.

Once a deal is completed, obviously you want to maintain a positive relationship with the new partner. It's also important to understand the driving factors that got the deal accomplished. Chris suggests making a "how the deal was done" memo documenting how long it took to get to milestones, key contacts, sticking points, what interested the prospect enough to become a partner, and other factors that influenced the completion of the deal. These memos help companies determine what's working in their process and what could be improved upon.

Business development has historically been a high-touch process that includes a lot of personal interactions. Reaching out to partners, understanding their needs, and negotiating terms are all part of a traditional business deal. However, businesses recently have been moving to more low-touch business development. Low-touch BD utilizes tools like application program interfaces (commonly known as APIs), feeds, crawling technology, and embed codes to reach new distribution channels and grow your influence. These methods allow you to standardize your value proposition and get more deals done.

Nevertheless, it still makes sense to land a few traditional deals first, and then transition to low-touch partnerships. Delicious's first key partnerships with Mozilla and *The Washington Post* happened in the traditional way. These partnerships generated significant traction for Delicious, so it made its API publicly available to the many sites that wanted to integrate with it. This required some up-front engineering work, but also meant that Delicious could now integrate with thousands of sites interested in leveraging its product.

Other companies have pursued low-touch business development in a similar way. SlideShare makes all slideshows embeddable, Disqus has its easy comment system installation, and SoundCloud makes its music library freely accessible. Such integrations fuel growth and vastly increase the pool of potential partners for a company.

However, just building a great API does not mean people will come and use it. Landing those first few partners through traditional means ensures that someone is getting value from working with your startup. Later, once you have more demand, you can start to standardize and simplify the partnership and integration process.

Whether you are starting out or scaling to millions of customers, business development can move the needle in any product phase. Kayak is a perfect example of this. It got its first customers through a key partnership with AOL. Later, Kayak partnered with hotel chains, rental agencies, and other groups to extend its reach to new groups of customers. The right deal at the right time can propel your company to the next phase of growth.

TARGETS

- **Pursue mutually beneficial partnerships.** In a standard partnership, two companies work together to make one or both of their products better by leveraging the unique capabilities of the other. Other major types of BD deals include partnerships focused on joint ventures, licensing, distribution, and inventory. You need to understand *why* a potential partner might want to work with you. What are their incentives? Just as you are evaluating potential partnerships in terms of your core metrics, they will be doing the same.
- **Focus on meeting your startup's core metrics.** Good business development deals align with your company and product

strategy and are focused on strategic product and distribution milestones. Avoid deals that don't directly align with your traction goal.

- **Create a pipeline of deals you're constantly working on.** For initial testing, you can reach out to a variety of potential partners to gauge interest.

CHAPTER EIGHTEEN

Sales

S ometimes hand-holding prospects can be necessary to turn them into real customers. One effective way to do that is via sales. Sales is the process of generating leads, qualifying them, and converting them into paying customers. This channel is particularly useful for enterprise and expensive products because often customers desire some form of inter-personal interaction before a purchase. Scaling this traction channel requires you to design and implement a repeatable sales model, which we cover in this chapter.

SALES STRATEGY

For consumer products, your first customers will likely come through channels other than sales—SEO, SEM, targeting blogs, and the like. When targeting bigger businesses, however, closing those first few critical customers can be significantly more challenging.

We interviewed Sean Murphy, owner of customer development and sales consulting firm SKMurphy, to talk about how he helps startups get their first enterprise customers:

> Most of the time [their first customer] is going to be somebody they know or we know. For the most part, our clients are going into a market that they understand with technology that they have developed. We help them make a list of every project they've worked on and everyone they've worked with. They reach out and say, "Here is what we are doing: do you know somebody we should talk to that makes sense?"
>
> People who've developed expertise by working in a field for a while are typically able to get an initial meeting—cup of coffee or lunch, these kinds of things. Sometimes we encourage them to shift to a different market because we find out that the technology has more applicability and offers more value there. One of the first things we help them with is what we call a lunch pitch. This is a single piece of paper that has five to ten bullets and perhaps a visual that helps them focus the conversation, making sure they understand the prospect's problem. The early conversations are all about exploring the prospect's problem and pain points.

Talking to prospects about their problems is not only a necessary sales tactic, but also necessary for good product development. John Raguin, cofounder of insurance software company Guidewire Software, explains:

> We went to our potential customers, insurance companies, and proposed to do a short free consulting study that would provide [an assessment] of their operation. We would spend approximately seven to ten man-days of effort understanding their operations, and at the end we would give them a high-level presentation benchmarking them as compared to their peers. In return, we asked for feedback on what would make the best system that would meet their needs. In the end, we

were able to work with over forty insurance companies this way. We were honest about our motives at all times, and we made sure to provide quality output.

When it comes to structuring your initial sales conversations, we suggest using the approach developed by Neil Rackham as outlined in his book *SPIN Selling*. It is a four-part question framework to use when talking to prospects, based on a decade spent researching 35,000 sales calls:

Situation questions. These questions help you learn about a prospect's buying situation. Typical questions include: *How many employees do you have?* and *How is your organization structured?*

> Ask only one or two of these questions per conversation, because the more situation questions a salesperson asks, the less likely he or she is to close a sale. That's because people feel like they're giving you information without getting anything in return. This is especially true of executive decision makers who are likely more pressed for time. Make sure you ask just enough situation questions to determine if you're talking to a likely candidate for a sale.

Problem questions. These are questions that clarify the buyer's pain points. *Are you happy with your current solution? What problems do you face with it?*

> Like situation questions, these questions should be used sparingly. You want to quickly define the problem they're facing so you can focus on the implications of this problem and how your solution helps.

Implication questions. These questions are meant to make a prospect aware of the implications that stem from the problem they're facing. These questions are based on information you uncovered while asking your problem questions. Questions could include: *Does this problem hurt your productivity? How many people does this issue impact, and in what ways? What customer or employee turnover are you experiencing because of this problem?*

> These questions should make your prospect feel the problem is larger and more urgent than he or she may have initially thought. For example, your prospect may see hard-to-use internal software as just an annoyance, a necessary cost of doing business. Implication questions can help shed light on the problems caused by this hard-to-use software: Does it lead to employee overtime because they struggle to accomplish things efficiently? Does it decrease overall quality of work? Does it impact employee turnover?

Each of the above questions helps frame the issue as a larger one in your prospect's mind. Then you transition to the final set of questions.

> **Need-payoff questions.** These questions focus attention on your solution and get buyers to think about the benefits of addressing the problem. Such questions should stem from the implication questions you asked earlier, and can include: *How do you feel this solution would help you? What type of impact would this have on you if we were to implement this within the next few months? Whose life would improve if this problem was solved, and how?*

The SPIN (Situation, Problem, Implication, Need-payoff) question model is a natural progression. First you clarify that the prospect is a potential customer and break the ice (situation questions). Then you get them talking about the problem (problem questions). Next, you uncover all the implications of this problem (implication questions). Finally, you focus on how your solution addresses these implications and will solve their problem (need-payoff questions).

How do you get your first customers? As Steve Barsh, former CEO of SECA (acquired by MCI), said in our interview, "You get your first customers by picking up the phone." If you are fortunate, you may be contacting people you know or were introduced to warmly by a friend. However, you may have to get your first customers by cold calling or emailing prospects.

We interviewed Todd Vollmer, an enterprise sales professional with more than twenty years of sales experience, who told us his approach to cold calling. Tactically, setting daily or weekly targets for outbound calls can help you get through the process. You'll be able to push yourself through some of those uncomfortable feelings (mainly stemming from rejections) with a concrete goal to work toward.

When making cold calls, be judicious about the people you contact. Cold calling junior employees is just as difficult mentally as calling more senior employees, but has a much lower success probability because they have less decision-making authority and industry knowledge. Sean Murphy suggests that your first interaction should be with employees who have some power, but aren't too high up:

> Ordinarily, it's somebody who is one level or two levels up in the organization; they've got enough perspective on the problem and on the organization to understand what's going to be involved in bringing change to the organization. As we work with them they may take us up the hierarchy to sell to more senior folks.
>
> We don't tend to start at the top unless we are calling on a very small business, in which case you've got to call on the CEO or one of the key execs because no one else can make any decisions.

Once you understand the potential customer's problem and you think your solution can help solve it, you can start to focus conversations on closing the customer. Specifically, Todd recommends getting answers for five specific areas:

Process—How does the company buy solutions like the one you're offering?
Need—How badly does this company need a solution like yours?

Authority—Which individuals have the authority to make the purchase happen?

Money—Do they have the funds to buy what you're selling? How much does *not* solving the problem cost them?

Estimated Timing—What are the budget and decision time lines for a purchase?

After a successful first call, Todd suggests sending a follow-up email documenting what you talked about, including the problems your prospect faces and the next steps. He also suggests closing emails with a direct question such as "Will you agree to this closing time line?"

Unfortunately, many enterprise entrepreneurs do not put enough thought into deciding on their first customer. Identifying the wrong first customer can lead to wasted time and squandered resources. Sean Murphy shared some pitfalls to avoid when seeking out a first customer:

> One [problem] occurs when the prospect invites you in . . . [but] has no interest in buying what you have or will develop. They would like to learn a lot about this emerging technology area, or this problem area, or something like that. . . .
>
> The second situation that's also a waste of time is when someone claims to be a "change agent." He will tell you that your offering is going to have a huge impact; it's going to transform all of General Motors, for example. Substitute your favorite lighthouse customer. Before you get started doing everything that he is telling you to do, you need to ask him, "Have you ever brought other technology into your company?" More often than not unfortunately he will say, "Well, no, but you know I've only been here six months, and this is what's going to let me make a big difference here."
>
> So the two typical problems are you end up giving away free consulting or you talk to somebody that in their own mind is this change agent, but they have no idea how to make it happen.

You want your first customers to be somewhat progressive and willing to work with you closely. As you're still developing your product, you want their active involvement in helping you craft the best solution. Forming a strong relationship is crucial because you want to use your first few customers as references and case studies to give your startup some measure of credibility when you start designing your sales funnel.

SALES TACTICS

Picture a funnel. As applied to sales, you start with many prospects at the top, quality the ones that make good customers in the middle, and then sell a certain number of them on your solution at the bottom. We interviewed David Skok, general partner at Matrix Partners and five-time entrepreneur (he's taken three companies public and one was acquired), to talk about creating profitable sales funnels.

The first goal is to drive leads into the top of the funnel. Usually, this means using other traction channels to make people aware of your product. While cold calling or emailing can be an effective way to reach your first customers, David believes it's less effective when trying to build a repeatable sales model:

> *I'm in favor of gaining traction through some kind of marketing channel first, then using sales as a conversion tool to close [those leads] into business. It's very, very expensive to use cold calling, and really not that effective by comparison with using marketing to get some kind of qualified prospect and then using sales to close that prospect.*

The next stage in a sales funnel is lead qualification. Here, you want to determine how ready a prospect is to buy, and if they're a prospect in which you should invest additional resources. For example, many companies require an email address and some company information in order to access materials on their site (e.g., a white paper or e-book). This information is then used to determine which prospects are worth spending more time on.

For example, HubSpot, which sells $5,000-plus-per-year marketing automation software, uses this information to determine how much time it should invest in a lead. If it gets a lead from someone running a small business on Etsy or eBay, HubSpot may choose to invest less time in that prospect because chances are someone running a smaller business is just not a good fit for its offering.

Mark Suster, two-time entrepreneur and partner at Upfront Ventures, suggests a simple approach to bucket leads into three categories: A's, B's, and C's:

> *I define "A deals" as those that have a realistic shot of closing in the next three months, "B deals" as those that you forecast to close within three to twelve months, and "C deals" as those that are unlikely to close within the next twelve months.*
>
> *"A deals" should get much of the salesperson's time (say 66 to 75 percent of time), "B deals" should get the balance as each sales rep needs to build their pipeline and bigger deals take time. And the key to scaling is that "C deals" should get no time from sales. They should be owned by marketing.*

In many organizations, marketing is in charge of generating leads and doing basic lead qualification. Then the sales team further qualifies and eventually closes the leads. It is part of the marketing department's job to make sure the sales team gets the information they need to just focus on qualified leads. Mark has this to say about marketing and sales working together:

> *Marketing's job in working with salespeople is twofold:*
>
> *To arm—which means to give the reps all of the sales collateral they'll need to effectively win sales campaigns. This includes presentations, ROI calculators, competitive analyses, and so forth.*
>
> *To aim—which means helping sales reps figure out which target customers to focus on. It's about helping weed out the nonserious leads from the urgent ones.*

Once you've qualified your leads, the final step is to create a purchase time line and convert prospects to paying customers. Todd recommends laying out exactly what you are going to do for the customer, setting up the timetable for it, and getting them to commit (with a "yes or no") to whether or not they will buy.

An agreement at this stage might look like this: "We'll set up a pilot system for you within two weeks. After two weeks, if you like the system we've built and it meets your needs, you'll buy from us. Yes or no?" Getting a yes or no answer allows you to focus your time on deals that are likely to close without wasting time on prospects that aren't prepared to buy.

Closing leads can happen in a variety of ways. For some products, it can be done completely by an inside sales team (meaning salespeople who don't travel). This team usually calls qualified leads, does a webinar or product demo, and has an ongoing email sequence that ends with a purchase request. In other cases, you may need a field sales team that actually visits prospective customers for some part of the process—it all depends on the complexity and length of your sales cycle.

Remember that, no matter how good your sales team, the customer is the one who decides to buy your product. It is crucial to keep the customer in mind as you design your sales funnel, meaning you should make their decision to buy as easy as possible. As David said in our interview:

> You want to recognize that your prospect has a series of issues and questions they will want resolved before they make a buying decision. These are things like "Am I sure that this is the best product?," "Am I sure that this will work for my situation?," "Will I get a good return on investment?," "Will this integrate with a system I have working in place today?," and so on.
>
> A lot of companies design their sales cycles around how they think things should work. I believe very strongly in the notion that you have to design it from the customer standpoint inwards, as opposed to your standpoint outwards, which is the normal way I see people thinking about this stuff.

Once you know what that buyer's questions are, you want to design your process to effectively address all of their questions and recognize what kinds of things need to be handled. Ideally, as many of these questions you can handle on your Web site, the better. Your job, once you have their email, is to answer all of their buying questions and then create a trigger that gives them a strong reason to buy.

You can keep track of when prospects are dropping out of your sales funnel. The points in your funnel where many prospects drop off are called "blockages."

Blockages are usually due to sales funnel complexity. You want to make purchasing your product as simple as possible. Some ways you can minimize blockages:

- Removing the need for IT installs with SaaS (Software as a Service)
- Free trials (including through open source software)
- Channel partners (resellers of your products)
- Demo videos
- FAQs
- Reference customers (such as testimonials or case studies)
- Email campaigns (where you educate prospective customers over time)
- Webinars or personal demos
- Easy installation and ease of use
- Low introductory price (less than $250/month for SMB, $10,000 for enterprises)
- Eliminating committee decision making

CASE STUDY: JBOSS

JBoss, an open source provider of middleware software, created a sales funnel that drove $65 million in revenue just two years after founding (Red Hat later acquired it for $350 million).

JBoss first focused on generating leads. More than 5 million people had downloaded its free software through SourceForge (a popular open source software directory), but JBoss had no contact information for these prospects. Knowing it needed a way to consistently generate leads, JBoss gave away its software's documentation (which it had previously charged for) in exchange for a customer's contact information.

This worked out well because customers were motivated to get the software documentation, which showed them how JBoss worked. Contact information was a small price to pay. For JBoss, this information was essential, as it could now communicate with prospects about its paid offerings. This tactic generated over more than ten thousand leads per month.

That many leads posed a problem of its own: the impossibility of contacting them all individually. It was now time for JBoss to qualify these leads and determine which were most likely to buy. The company used Eloqua, marketing automation software, to determine the pages and links a prospect engaged with before accessing the documentation. Prospects who spent a lot of time on support pages were good candidates for the JBoss support service, the product that generates revenue for the company.

JBoss's marketing team would call these promising leads to further qualify them. Each of these calls was made specifically to determine if a prospect had the desire to get a deal done. If so, qualified prospects were passed to sales.

In this final stage of the funnel, prospects were contacted by individuals from an inside sales team. This is where the standard sales process kicks in: calls, demos, white papers, etc. The sales team closed about 25 percent of these prospects thanks to their thorough lead qualification (industry averages hover between 7 and 10 percent).

Unqualified leads not yet ready for sales were put into lead nurturing campaigns. These prospects received the *JBoss Newsletter*, as well as invitations to webinars, and were encouraged to subscribe to the JBoss blog. Customers who reached a certain level of interaction with nurturing campaigns (e.g., those who clicked on certain links in emails or attended a webinar) would then be put back into the sales pipeline and contacted by someone from sales.

JBoss built an impressive and wildly successful sales funnel. A big reason for JBoss's success was that its sales funnel was designed from the standpoint of the customer. The company utilized free tools to generate leads at a low cost by offering customers the documentation they wanted in exchange for contact information. It then qualified them through marketing built on internal analytics. Finally, JBoss used an inside sales team to close each deal at an average deal size above $10,000.

TARGETS

- **Don't rule out cold calling.** Good first customers have a burning need to address a problem, are interested in your approach to solving their problem, and are willing to work with you closely. Sometimes cold calling is the only way to find them.
- **Build a repeatable sales model.** An effective sales funnel has prospects enter at the top, qualifies these leads, and closes them effectively. Map out your sales funnel, identify blockages, and remove them. Keep the buying process as simple as possible.
- **Get the buyer to commit to time lines.** To close sales effectively, get an affirmative at each point that you are on track to close. Always know exactly what steps are left.
- **Keep the customer's perspective in mind.** Talk to people who *need* your product and understand their common concerns. Address those concerns specifically on your Web site.

CHAPTER NINETEEN
Affiliate Programs

An affiliate program is an arrangement where you pay people or companies for performing certain actions like making a sale or getting a qualified lead. For example, a blogger may recommend a product and take a cut when there are sales through her blog. In this case the blogger is the affiliate.

Companies like Amazon, Zappos, eBay, Orbitz, and Netflix use affiliate programs to drive significant portions of their revenue. In fact, affiliate programs are the core traction channel for many e-commerce stores, information products, and membership programs.

For this channel, we interviewed Kris Jones, founder of the Pepperjam affiliate network, which was acquired by eBay in 2009. Kris grew Pepperjam to become the fourth largest affiliate network in the world: at one point, it had a *single advertiser* generating *$50 million* annually through its network.

AFFILIATE PROGRAM STRATEGY

Affiliate programs are frequently found in retail, information products, and lead generation.

Retail affiliate programs facilitate the purchase of tangible products and account for more than $2 billion annually. Amazon, Target, and Walmart have the biggest programs and pay affiliates a percentage of each sale they make. Amazon's affiliate program, for example, pays between 4 and 8.5 percent of each sale depending on how many items an affiliate sells each month.

Some large retailers like Amazon and eBay run their own affiliate programs, but this is rare. These programs involve recruiting, managing, and paying thousands of affiliates, which is too complex and expensive for most companies to manage themselves. It is much more convenient for online retailers to go through existing retail affiliate networks.

Sites like Commission Junction (CJ), Pepperjam, and LinkShare all have strong networks of affiliates that make a living promoting others' products. The list of companies that take advantage of these networks contains the most recognizable names in the retail industry: Walmart, Apple, Starbucks, The North Face, The Home Depot, Verizon, Best Buy, and many others.

The affiliates that join these programs vary widely, but generally fall into the following major categories:

Coupon/deal sites. These sites—RetailMeNot, CouponCabin, Brad's Deals, and Slickdeals to name a few—offer discounts to visitors and take a cut of any sale that occurs. For example, when you search for "Zappos discount," RetailMeNot is likely to rank highly for that search term. When you visit the RetailMeNot page that comes up, you get coupon codes for Zappos. If you click through and buy something using a code, RetailMeNot gets a percentage.

Loyalty programs. Companies like Upromise and Ebates have reward programs that offer cash back on purchases made through their partner networks. They earn money based on the amount their members spend through retail affiliate programs. For example, if a thousand members buy gift certificates to Olive Garden, Upromise will get a percentage of every dollar spent. Then they pay part of what they earn back to their members.

Aggregators. Sites such as Nextag and PriceGrabber aggregate products from retailers. They often add information to product listings, like additional ratings or price comparisons.

Email lists. Many affiliates have large email lists to which they will recommend products. They then take a cut when subscribers make purchases.

Vertical sites. Hundreds of thousands of sites (including individual blogs) have amassed significant audiences geared toward a vertical, such as parenting, sports, or electronics.

Information products include digital products like e-books, software, music, and (increasingly) education. Since it doesn't cost anything to make another digital copy, selling info products through affiliate programs is quite popular. Creators will give large percentages to affiliates that promote their products.

By far the largest affiliate network for information products is ClickBank, where affiliate commissions often reach 75 percent. ClickBank has more than 100,000 affiliates and millions of products.

Lead generation is a $26 billion industry. Insurance companies, law firms, and mortgage brokers all pay hefty commissions to get customer leads. Depending on the industry, a lead may include a working email address, home address, or phone number. It may also include more qualifying information like a credit score.

Affiliate programs are popular with financial services and insurance companies because the value of each customer is so high. Think of how much you spend on auto or health insurance annually: that should give you a sense of why a lead is so valuable. In fact, insurance companies are top Google AdWords spenders, often paying $50 to $100 for a single click!

These companies often create their own affiliate programs or go through popular lead-gen networks like Affiliate.com, Clickbooth, Neverblue, and Adknowledge.

AFFILIATE PROGRAM TACTICS

Your ability to use affiliate programs effectively depends on how much you are willing to pay to acquire a customer. After all, with this channel you are paying out of pocket for the lead or sale.

We recommend going through an existing affiliate network—something like Commission Junction, Pepperjam, ShareASale, or more specific networks targeted at your type of product. Using a network makes it easier to recruit affiliates because so many are already signed up on these sites. It allows you to start using this traction channel immediately. Otherwise, you'd have to first recruit affiliates on your own, which takes significant time and money.

Setting up an affiliate program on one of these existing affiliate networks is relatively easy, though it does require an up-front cost. In the case of Commission Junction, that cost is more than $2,000. However, if you successfully recruit high-performing affiliates through the network, affiliate sales will quickly cover the initial fee.

The other option is to build your own affiliate program independent of an existing network. With such a program, you recruit partners from your customer base or people who have access to a group of customers you want to reach.

One benefit of this approach is you don't have to pay your affiliates all in cash. Instead, you can use the features of your product as currency. For example, if your startup has a freemium business model, you could give away certain features or extend subscriptions. Earlier, we explained how Dropbox's referral program involves giving people free storage space. Another example is QuiBids, a top penny auction site. It built out a referral program for its current customers that gives free bids to people who refer other customers.

The first place to look for potential affiliates is your own customer base.

They are easy to recruit and work with because they are already familiar with and have an affinity for your brand.

After getting customers involved in your affiliate program, you will want to contact content creators, including bloggers, publishers, social media influencers, and email list curators. Monetizing blogs can be difficult, so these content creators often look for other ways to make money.

We interviewed Maneesh Sethi, popular blogger at HacktheSystem, to talk about how companies can build relationships with people like him. Maneesh has been an affiliate for many products he has personally used. As an example, Maneesh was a customer of a program that taught SEO tactics. He loved the program, so he contacted the company himself and worked out a deal with them to give him a commission for each new customer he sent their way. After agreeing to terms, Maneesh sent out an email to his list mentioning how the SEO program had helped him get better rankings on Google. That single offer has made him nearly $30,000 in two years, and has made the company much more.

Maneesh also has recommended RescueTime, a time-tracking application that helps you be more productive. As one of its top affiliates, he has referred more than three thousand people to the product since he joined its affiliate program. Through Maneesh, RescueTime was able to reach a new audience without spending a lot of money on marketing or wasting it on leads that didn't convert.

Maneesh mentioned that the best way to reach someone like him is by building a relationship: help the content creators where you can, writing guest posts or granting free access to your product. In turn, they'll be happy to promote you if you have a truly great product.

Well-established affiliate programs like those run by Amazon or Netflix have figured out exactly how much to pay their affiliates for each lead. As a startup, you are going to be less sure of your underlying business and should start with a simple approach. The simplest approaches are to pay a flat fee for a conversion (e.g., $5 for a customer who purchases something) or to pay a percentage of a conversion that occurs (e.g., 5 percent of the price a customer pays).

More established affiliate programs get more complex by segmenting products and rewarding top affiliates. eBay gives seasonal coupon codes to its affiliates for product categories it wants to push. Tiered payout programs are also popular. In this structure, affiliates get paid a percentage (or flat fee) of each transaction. The percentage is based on the number of sales you make—if you drive more transactions, your rate goes up, and you make more money.

Major Affiliate Networks

Here are the top affiliate networks, as well as a list of software tools that can help you build your own referral program without a substantial engineering investment.

Commission Junction—CJ has many of the largest Internet retailers on its platform. It is also somewhat pricey: it costs upward of $2,000 to sell your product through its network. This high cost, combined with the fact that CJ curates both affiliates and publishers for performance, creates a high level of quality in its network.

ClickBank—The leading platform for anyone selling digital products online (courses, e-books, digital media). ClickBank is relatively cheap to start with, as you need to pay only $50 to list a product on its platform.

Affiliate.com—Affiliate.com promises a very strict affiliate approval process, which it claims means higher-quality traffic for its advertisers.

Pepperjam—Started by Kris Jones (whom we interviewed for this chapter), the Pepperjam Exchange encompasses multiple channels (mobile, social, offline retail, print, etc.). Pepperjam promotes its customer support and transparency as selling points for its network, which costs $1,000 to join.

ShareASale—This affiliate network has more than 2,500 merchants and allows advertisers to be flexible in determining commission structures. It costs about $500 to get started.

Adknowledge—Adknowledge offers traditional ad-buying services in addition to affiliate campaigns. It also works in mobile, search, social media, and display advertising, giving advertisers access to affiliate and CPC outlets through one platform.

LinkShare—LinkShare helps companies find affiliates and builds lead-gen programs for them. Companies like Macy's, Avon, and Champion use them to manage affiliate programs.

MobAff—MobAff is a mobile affiliate network that utilizes SMS, push notifications, click to call, mobile display, and mobile search to drive conversions for its advertisers.

Neverblue—Neverblue is targeted toward advertisers that spend more than $20,000 per month. It also works with its advertising partners on their advertisements and campaigns. It counts Groupon, eHarmony, and Vistaprint as some of its clients.

Clickbooth—Clickbooth uses search, email, and many Web sites to promote brands like DirecTV, Dish Network, and QuiBids.

RetailMeNot, Inc. (formerly WhaleShark Media)—This media company owns some of the most popular coupon sites in the world, including RetailMeNot and Deals2Buy.com. Companies can partner with RetailMeNot to drive coupon-based affiliate transactions through its sites, which often appear near the top of Google for any "term + coupon" search.

CONCLUSION

Kris stressed that more startups should take advantage of this traction channel. As he put it:

> *For startups that don't have a lot of money, where you can't just open a PPC [pay-per-click] account and start throwing darts, affiliate marketing seems to me to be a logical place to start.*
>
> *There's really no guarantee that if you spend $10,000 on Google AdWords you'll make more than that. If you were to*

compare affiliate marketing and PPC, the advertiser assumes the risk in PPC. If you set up poorly written and poorly thought out campaigns on AdWords, you're going to have to pay for the click whether or not your ads suck, or whether or not they're converting well.

With affiliate marketing, you get to define what the transaction or the conversion is, and you also have tools available to mitigate low quality. For instance, if someone refers an e-commerce transaction to you but the credit card is declined, the affiliate commission is zero. If someone submits a lead form, but the lead doesn't follow the rules you set out (a legitimate email address, a real postal address, etc.), you don't have to pay for that. You don't assume the risk.

TARGETS

- **Test using an existing affiliate network.** It already has affiliates, so you can start using this traction channel immediately.
- **Keep your payouts simple.** Know how much you can spend to acquire a customer and keep it below that. As you get deeper into this channel you can test more complicated payout programs.
- **The next place you should look for more affiliates is your customers.** They already like you, and so there may be a lot of them willing to sell for you.

CHAPTER TWENTY

Existing Platforms

Existing platforms are Web sites, apps, or networks with huge numbers of users—sometimes in the hundreds of millions—that you can potentially leverage to get traction. Major platforms include the Apple and Android app stores, Mozilla and Chrome browser extensions, social platforms like Facebook, Twitter, and Pinterest, as well as newer platforms that are growing rapidly (Tumblr, Snapchat, etc.).

When mobile video-sharing app Socialcam launched, it suggested users sign up with Facebook or Twitter, promoted user videos on both platforms, and encouraged people to invite their friends from each site. It went on to hit 60 million users within twelve months—that type of growth just isn't possible through many other channels.

EXISTING PLATFORMS STRATEGY: APP STORES

With the number of smartphone users well above one billion and growing every day, we've seen an explosion of apps reaching millions of users in short periods of time: months, rather than years.

The most efficient way for an app to get discovered in the app stores is through the top app rankings and featured listings sections. These rankings group apps by category, country, popularity, and editors' choice. The story of Trainyard illustrates the impact an App Store feature can have.

Trainyard, a paid iOS game developed by Matt Rix, wasn't growing the way he had hoped. Because free applications are downloaded at a much higher rate than paid, app developers will often release a free version and monetize those free users via in-app purchases or paid upgrades.

Matt decided to try this tactic. When he released the free version of Trainyard (Trainyard Express), an editor at a popular Italian blog wrote a glowing piece on it almost immediately. This propelled the app to be the number-one free app in Italy—netting more than 22,000 downloads on that day alone! The app then hit the top spot in the United Kingdom and was downloaded more than 450,000 times in a week.

Seven days after that, Apple decided to feature it. Everything that happened before was dwarfed by what happened next. Downloads skyrocketed by 50x and persisted at those heightened levels while the feature was live. Millions of downloads. And even after the feature passed, daily download levels remained significantly elevated compared with where they were before.

Trainyard illustrates the importance of getting enough attention for your app so that it shows up in the rankings and featured sections. Mark Johnson, founder of Focused Apps LLC, wrote about how app promotions usually work:

1. *Ads get the [app] somewhere into the charts.*
2. *Now it's in the charts, more people see it.*
3. *So it gets more organic downloads.*
4. *Which makes it go a bit higher up in the charts.*
5. *Now even more people see it and it gets more organic downloads.*
6. *People like it and start telling their friends to get it too.*
7. *It goes up higher in the charts.*
8. *Repeat from 5.*

Companies use many tactics to get into the charts initially. They buy ads from places like AdMob, buy installs from companies like Tapjoy, cross-promote their apps (through cross-promotion networks or other apps they own), or even buy their way to the top of the charts through services like FreeAppADay.

Other traction channels can also drive adoption of your mobile app: as Trainyard showed, the publicity and targeting blogs channels can work well. While none of these tactics are enough on their own, they can help you get the ball rolling toward a ranking or feature.

However, for top rankings to happen sustainably, you need to have a compelling app that is rated highly on a regular basis. Ratings matter a lot—they influence individual choices to download an app, editors choose apps to feature based on them, and they're often mentioned in any press coverage. That's why you see even top apps continually asking you to rate them.

There are some tricks you can use, like asking people to rate your app right after you give them something useful, but really the base experience has to be excellent to get consistently high rankings. Even with hundreds of thousands of apps, there are shockingly few that are truly amazing user experiences. Most of the apps that are now household names—Instagram, Path, Google Maps, Pandora, Spotify—all have excellent user experiences and consistently high ratings.

Browser extensions in Chrome and add-ons in Firefox are apps you can download for your Web browser. The most popular browser extension is Adblock Plus, which blocks ads on major Web sites. Other popular extensions help you download YouTube videos, save bookmarks across computers, and manage your passwords.

Web users visit dozens of different sites every day; to establish yours as a site they consistently visit can be difficult. A browser add-on allows people to get value from your product without consistently returning to your site.

Evernote, a memory-enhancement and productivity tool, saw a huge jump in customers when it launched its browser extensions. In its "2010

Year in Review" blog post, Evernote said Web usage went up 205 percent thanks to these extensions—and this from a company with more than 6 million users at the time!

Like mobile app stores, browser extensions have dedicated portals where you download the apps, though unlike app stores, all the apps are free. These portals also have features and rankings, which you should be similarly seeking if you focus on this area.

EXISTING PLATFORMS STRATEGY: SOCIAL SITES

The use of social sites is constantly shifting as people change where they communicate online. Newer social platforms like Snapchat and Vine are adding users at a dizzying pace, and we're sure others will follow them soon.

Even though keeping up with the evolution of social platforms can be challenging, they remain one of the best ways to rapidly acquire large numbers of customers. In fact, it makes sense to focus on platforms that are just taking off.

Social platforms that haven't fully matured also haven't built all of the features they'll eventually need; you might be able to fill in one of those gaps. They also are less saturated, as larger brands are often slower to target up-and-coming sites.

YouTube got its initial traction by filling gaps in the Myspace platform. In the mid-2000s Myspace was the most visited social networking site in the world. Video sharing on the Web wasn't user friendly yet—it was difficult to upload videos and put them on other sites.

Myspace didn't have a native video hosting solution. YouTube stepped in and provided one that was simple: you could upload and embed a video in Myspace in a matter of minutes. Even better for YouTube, Myspace users were directed *back* to YouTube when they clicked on the embedded videos. This exposed many Myspace users to all of the great features and content available on YouTube, and was responsible for YouTube's rapid early growth.

Every major platform has similar stories. Bitly fulfilled the need to share shortened links on Twitter and saw most of its adoption from such use. Imgur built its image-hosting solution for reddit users, and has seen an explosion in usage as a result. This pattern repeats itself time and time again.

There are thousands of other large sites and marketplaces that you can target to get customers. First, figure out where your potential customers hang out online. Then create a strategy to target potential customers on these existing platforms. Sites like Amazon, eBay, Craigslist, Tumblr, GitHub, and Behance have all helped startups build traction.

Airbnb saw much of its early growth come through Craigslist. Customers who used Craigslist found that Airbnb was a much simpler and safer solution. With this knowledge, the company's engineers developed a "Post to Craigslist" feature that would allow you to list your bed on Craigslist. Though this feature eventually was shut down, it drove tens of thousands of Craigslist users back to Airbnb to book a room.

PayPal, the leading online payments platform, used a similar strategy when it targeted eBay users as its first customers. In the beginning, PayPal itself purchased goods from eBay and required that the sellers accept payment through PayPal. This worked so well that PayPal proved more popular than the payment system eBay itself was trying to implement! This single-minded focus allowed PayPal to acquire a large percentage of people within one of the few groups of buyers and sellers that dealt with online payments at the time.

CASE STUDY: EVERNOTE

Since its founding, Evernote has focused on existing platforms as its core traction channel. We talked with Alex Pachikov, on the founding team of Evernote. His company was recently valued at over one billion dollars.

Evernote has made it a priority to be on every new and existing platform. It benefits from the platform's initial marketing push and increases its chances of getting featured. As Evernote's CEO, Phil Libin, puts it:

> We really killed ourselves in the first couple of years to always
> be in all of the App Store launches on day one. Whenever a
> new device or platform would come out, we would work day

and night for months before that to make sure Evernote was there and supporting the new device or operating system in the App Store on the first day. . . .

When iPhone launched we were one of the very first iPhone apps, so we were promoted and had a lot of visibility. When iPad launched, we were there on day one, not just with a port of our iPhone client, which a lot of other companies did. . . . [We had] a completely new designed version for the iPad even though we'd never seen an iPad before—we stood in line with everyone else. Same thing with Android devices and the Kindle Fire.

Being first can open you up to the opportunity to benefit from the early marketing and promotion about the platform itself. As Alex said:

Every year there's a new platform, new device, new something, and as somebody who's starting a company you should consider if there's something really cool you can do on an upcoming platform. Now obviously you can't plan if a platform is going to be successful, but you can [make some] reasonable guesses based on past experiences with a company.

I think people see this as gambling. People take the "I will support this platform when it has a million users" type of approach. That's a fine thing to do if you are EA or Adobe or something like that. And maybe for Evernote a year from now, that's the right thing to do. But for a startup, you really aren't in that position. When a platform is popular, it's crowded. . . . A lot of people have cool apps and could do really, really well if they were to get this initial push, and that initial push is free if you do it early. But you risk that all that effort is a waste.

Evernote was one of the first apps available for Android. Because it had some very cool functionality, it was featured in the Android store for six weeks straight, at a time when it was far less crowded than it is now. This gave Evernote hundreds of thousands of new customers, all because it was early and focused its engineering efforts on being first on the platform. Similarly, when Verizon picked up Android phones, Evernote benefited from the national marketing push Verizon did to promote its Android launch.

This build-early strategy doesn't work in every case, especially when the underlying platform flops. Evernote took the same approach with the Nokia, Windows, and BlackBerry smartphone platforms, none of which moved the needle. Nevertheless, Alex is very happy with the overall strategy: when it works—as with Android—it more than makes up for the failures.

In the last few years, Evernote's strategy has been to expand beyond its pure note-taking app and release many different apps for specific verticals (Evernote Food for food notes, Evernote Hello for remembering people, etc.). Because getting promoted in app stores has been its most effective growth tactic, this strategy enables Evernote to get featured and ranked in categories where Evernote's main app does not appear.

At Evernote, Alex mentioned that they think hard about what types of features or apps would stand out to editors:

> *You have to think ahead. What types of things would Apple or Google really like? What are things that, if we were to do, Apple or Google or Microsoft would be looking for? And is there a natural fit between what we do and what they would be looking for?*

This thought process has led to apps like Evernote Peek. Peek was an app that allowed you to turn your media (notes, videos, or audio) into study material that you interacted with using the iPad Smart Cover. While now discontinued, it felt magical at the time because it took advantage of a new Apple technology. It was so cool that Apple itself showcased it in a commercial!

Peek was featured in Apple's education category, and was the number-one educational app for over a month. This exposure led to more than

500,000 new Evernote users who experienced the product through Peek, and was one of the strongest growth drivers for the company during 2012.

Though Evernote has seen most of its growth come through mobile channels, its platform strategy works perfectly well on nonmobile platforms. The important takeaway is that it is a good idea to focus on new and untapped platforms to generate growth. Chris Dixon, a partner at Andreessen Horowitz and the founder of Hunch before its acquisition by eBay, had this to say about platform-based growth:

> Some of the most successful startups grew by making bets on emerging platforms that were not yet saturated and where barriers to discovery were low. . . . Betting on new platforms means you'll likely fail if the platform fails, but it also dramatically lowers the distribution risks described above.

TARGETS

- **Figure out where your potential customers are hanging out online.** They could be on major platforms, on niche platforms, or on some combination thereof. Then embark on a strategy to target these existing platforms.
- **Create a feature specifically to fill a gap for that platform's users.** Large companies have been built on the back of each major social platform by filling gaps with features that the platform was not providing itself.
- **Focus on new and untapped platforms.** Or try new aspects of major platforms because there is less competition there.

CHAPTER TWENTY-ONE

Trade Shows

Trade shows offer you the opportunity to showcase your products in person. These events are often exclusive to industry insiders, and are designed to foster interactions between vendors and their prospects.

Early on, you can use this traction channel to build interest in what you're building. As you get more established, you can use trade shows as an opportunity to make a major announcement, sell big clients, seal a partnership, or as an integral part of your sales funnel.

We interviewed Brian Riley of SureStop, the company behind the SureStop bike brake. His startup has used trade shows to gain traction at every phase, from preproduct to a major distribution deal with a large bike manufacturer. We also spoke with Jason Cohen, founder of WP Engine, who used trade show marketing at his first company, Smart Bear Software.

TRADE SHOW STRATEGY

Almost every industry has a large number of trade shows: the tough part is deciding which ones to attend. The best way to decide whether to exhibit at an event is to visit as a guest and do a walkthrough the year before. Attending as a guest allows you to get a feel for an event without straining your budget. If this isn't possible, the next best option is to get the opinions of people who have exhibited at previous shows: *How crowded was it? How high was the quality of attendees? Would you go again?* These are important questions that will help you decide if a particular trade show is right for your startup.

Brad Feld, a partner at Foundry Group, suggests following these steps when deciding which events to pick:

- Set your goals for attending trade shows this year. For example, are you trying to get press, lure investors, land major customers, work out significant partnerships, or something else? Your goals should drive your decisions about which events to attend and how to approach them.
- Write down all events in your industry.
- Next, evaluate each event in the context of your goals. In particular, think about the type of interactions you want and whether these interactions take place at each event. For example, if you need to have long conversations with prospects to do customer development, seek out an event with an intimate atmosphere. If your goal is to interact with as many potential customers as possible, a crowded event would be a better fit.
- Figure out how much you can spend per year and allocate this budget by quarter. This allows you to align events on your schedule with your budget while also giving you flexibility to reallocate in later quarters if company goals change.
- Finally, work backward to see if attending a particular event makes sense given your quarterly budget. For example, let's say you are attending Traction Trade Show and your goal is to

increase sales. When you receive the attendee list from the conference organizer (ask for it if it is not provided), you see that ten thousand people are going. However, you estimate that only 30 percent of those people fit the profile of a potential customer, so the total number of people you can realistically target is three thousand. If it will cost you $10,000 to attend this trade show and the price of your product is $5,000, it may make sense for you to attend. That is, your trip will be profitable around the third sale with these numbers. Then the decision comes down to what other traction opportunities you have right now. However, if you are selling a $50 product, you probably won't sell enough to make attending this trade show worth your while.

SureStop attended a few trade shows early on with prototypes on hand—no manufacturing line, no pricing, and no concrete plans to sell anything yet. Their goal was simply to have conversations with other companies about the features they wanted to see in SureStop's products.

From these conversations, they learned what their product needed from a technical standpoint and the price points they needed to hit. Later, when they had developed a product, they increased their presence and expenses at trade shows. In other words, as their company goals changed, their actions at each show changed with them.

TRADE SHOW TACTICS

Your preparation for a trade show will determine how successful you will be. This is one of the few times during the year when nearly everyone in your industry is in one place; you'll want to be at your best.

To prepare, make a list of key attendees you want to meet at the trade show. Then schedule meetings with them before you attend the event. Brian sent well-researched emails explaining what SureStop did and how its technology could benefit the people he wanted to meet. He also attached a one-pager with more information about the company. This strategy allowed him to meet the people he wanted at every event he attended.

Jason Cohen put it this way:

Set up meetings. Yes, meetings! Trade shows are a rare chance to get face time with:

- *Editors of online and offline magazines. Often overlooked, editors are your key to real press. I've been published in every major programming magazine; almost all of that I can directly attribute to talking with editors at trade shows! It works.*
- *Bloggers you like, especially if you wish they'd write about you.*
- *Existing customers.*
- *Potential customers currently trialing your stuff.*
- *Your vendors.*
- *Your competition.*
- *Potential partners.*

Proactively set meetings. Call/email everyone you can find. It's easy to use email titles which will be obviously non-spam such as "At [Trade Show X]: Can we chat for 5 minutes?" I try to get at least five meetings per day. Organizing dinner and/or drinks after the show is good too.

If publicity is one of your goals, reach out to media that will be in attendance. Media members attend trade shows *specifically* to see what's going on in an industry—give them something to write about! This could be a new product, feature, or deal with a big customer.

Successful trade shows come down to the relationships you build and the impression you make on journalists, prospective customers, and potential partners. Mark Suster, partner at Upfront Ventures, suggests hosting dinners for such people to strengthen these relationships:

The other secret conference trick that is orchestrated by the true Zen masters is to schedule a dinner and invite other people. It's a great way to get to know people intimately. Start by booking a few easy-to-land friends who are interesting. Work hard to bag a "brand name" person who others will want to meet. All it takes is one. Then the rest of your invites can mention that person's name on the guest list (name others, too . . . obviously) and you will be able to draw in some other people you'd like to meet.

Another similar strategy is with customers. If you invite three to four customers and three to four prospects to a dinner with two or three employees and some other interesting guests you'll be doing well. Potential customers always prefer to talk to existing reference customers than to talk to just your sales reps.

Final tip: picking a killer venue is one of the best ways to bag high-profile people. Everybody loves to eat somewhere hot. However, sometimes a dinner can be too expensive for an early-stage company. So why not go in on the dinner with two other companies? That way you're all extending your networks and splitting the costs.

When planning your booth, first determine where you want to be located on the show floor. If your goal is to reach many attendees (as opposed to targeting a few high-value prospects), you need visibility. That means you want a booth in a well-trafficked location and a marketing plan to get people to take notice. If your strategy is dependent on talking to just a few key partners, a great booth location and the added cost that comes with it doesn't make as much sense. In fact, you may want to be situated in a very particular place, such as next to a specific established company.

No matter what your location, you will want to put together an impressive display. Having a big banner that says what you do, nice-looking booth materials, business cards, and a compelling demo are the basics. If that seems like a lot to put together, there are many vendors that help companies create trade show materials.

To attract people to his startup's booth, Jason Cohen, founder of Smart Bear Software, would send out discount cards for its software to all attendees before the actual conference. The recipients had to come to his booth to redeem the discounts.

Giveaways are an important way of getting some buzz and inbound traffic at a trade show. Coffee mugs and stress balls are tried and true, but you can get even more creative with more unique items (yo-yos, coconuts, cigar cutters) to stand out during the show. A play on the name of your company or your core value proposition gets people talking about your booth. For example, DuckDuckGo could give out duck key chains or sunglasses to showcase that they don't track your searches.

You can also be proactive on the trade show floor to bring people back to your booth. The founders of RJMetrics, a business analytics subscription service, told us about how they've had success starting conversations by walking up to people at trade shows:

> One thing was clear: it pays to have an outbound strategy. Only 28 percent of our conversations were walk-ups. This means that employing an outbound strategy allowed us to extract between three and four times as much value from the show as we would have otherwise.

A proactive and inexpensive method that requires no creativity is giving away as many bags with your company's name on it as possible. Most attendees travel with armloads of pamphlets, catalogs, flyers, and giveaways. Stopping each to offer them a bag to put it in gets them talking to you but, more important, gets your name displayed all over the conference area.

Many companies also do something particularly engaging within their booths to get people to stay there long enough to experience their full pitch. SureStop has a funny video demo comparing its brakes with the regular brakes found on bikes. The video shows an individual using regular bike brakes speeding down a mountain and braking and promptly getting thrown over the handlebars. Then, as a comparison, the same person in the same scenario is shown using a bike with SureStop brakes and comes to a quick, safe stop. It's a simple and compelling way to pique people's interest in the product.

When you do engage a person, each of the materials you give out should have a specific call to action (CTA). For example, if someone picked up a business card at your booth, it should have an enticing offer (e.g., download a free industry guide), along with a unique link to that download. Make sure this page is mobile optimized, as most of your visitors will be accessing the page from a mobile device.

One step beyond hosting dinners is throwing a party near the show center. Like dinners, these are a great way to loosen up and chat with others at the event. You could cosponsor these with other startups to keep costs reasonable.

Trade shows give you more direct interaction with customers, partners, and press in a short period of time than most other traction channels. Those connections can be especially valuable if your key customers and partners are geographically diverse, and traveling to meet each of them separately would be prohibitively expensive. This channel has the potential to move the needle in a matter of days.

That's what happened with SureStop. After a major industry trade show, they managed to form a relationship with Jamis, one of the largest players in the bike manufacturing industry. They met Jamis early on, when they had just a prototype. From that meeting, SureStop learned the necessary specifications they'd need to have if they wanted to work with Jamis.

After SureStop built its product to those specs, SureStop formed a manufacturing relationship with Jamis. Its brakes are now stopping thousands of bikes nationwide, and are its biggest source of traction. And all of it started and grew through this traction channel.

TARGETS

- **Schedule meetings and dinners ahead of time.** Identify your top targets and find a way to engage them individually at the show.

- **Investigate the efficacy of shows before committing.** Attend shows this year you might want to exhibit at next year. Reach out to previous exhibitors.
- **Have an inbound and outbound strategy for your booth.** Do something proactive and creative. Include a strong call to action on every item you give out.

CHAPTER TWENTY-TWO
Offline Events

S ponsoring or running offline events—from small meetups to large conferences—can be a primary way to get traction. Twilio, a tool that makes it easy to add phone calls and text messaging to apps, attracts its customers by sponsoring hackathons, conferences, and meetups, large and small. Larger companies like Oracle and Box throw huge events to maintain their position as market leaders. Salesforce's Dreamforce conference has more than 100,000 attendees!

In phase I, offline events give you the opportunity to engage directly with potential customers about their problems. Such events are especially important when your target customers do not respond well to online advertising and do not have a natural place to congregate online. Attracting these customers to one location or going to a place where they meet in person can be the most effective way to reach them.

Offline events are particularly effective for startups with long sales cycles, as is often the case with enterprise software. We'll look at how Enservio reached decision makers and shortened its sales cycle by using this channel. You can also use offline events to build relationships with power users, as both Yelp and Evite have done successfully.

OFFLINE EVENTS STRATEGY

Conferences are the biggest and most popular type of offline event. Each year hundreds of startup-related conferences and thousands of business conferences are held worldwide.

You can benefit from a conference in any startup phase. In phase I, where smaller groups of people can move the needle, attending meetups and events is a prime way to do so. Tech startups in phase II can take advantage of larger tech conferences like TechCrunch Disrupt, Launch Conference, and SXSW to build on their existing traction. Twitter launched nine months before SXSW in 2007 and was seeing decent amounts of traction, on the order of several thousand users. Because many of its early users were headed to SXSW, Twitter saw the conference as an opportunity to accelerate its adoption. As Twitter cofounder Evan Williams said:

> We did two things to take advantage of the emerging critical mass:
>
> 1. We created a Twitter visualizer and negotiated with the festival to put flat panel screens in the hallways. . . . We paid $11K for this and set up the TVs ourselves. (This was about the only money Twitter's ever spent on marketing.)
>
> 2. We created an event-specific feature where you could text "join sxsw" to 40404. Then you would show up on the screens. And, if you weren't already a Twitter user, you'd automatically be following a half dozen or so "ambassadors," who were Twitter users also at SXSW. We advertised this on the screens in the hallways.

Thanks to this conference-specific marketing, Twitter jumped from twenty thousand tweets per day to more than sixty thousand by the end of the conference. Twitter also won the SXSW Web Award, leading to press coverage and even more awareness of its service.

Eric Ries wanted to broaden the audience for the Lean Startup principles he was promoting on his blog. However, he was afraid his message would get lost at a large conference like SXSW. Instead, he organized his own conference and invited founders of successful companies to talk about how Lean principles worked in their startups.

First, Eric tested demand for his conference by asking his readers if they would be interested in such an event. After a resounding yes, he sold conference tickets through his site and other popular startup blogs.

Startup Lessons Learned began as a one-day conference in San Francisco with just a few speakers and panels focused on Lean Startup concepts. The short event was attractive to individuals who didn't want to spend a lot on travel or take time off work. In addition, Eric avoided the extra cost and coordination headaches that come with arranging a multiday event: flying in speakers, hotel stays, and so on. He made the commitment to attend as simple as possible. The result was a strong turnout and a great conference experience.

While he didn't want people to have to travel to attend, he still wanted people from out of the area to find out what was happening at the conference. To this end, Eric live-streamed the conference to meetup groups across the country. The people who attended those meetups or watched on individual live streams were instrumental in promoting his ideas to a larger audience and making his book a bestseller.

Other companies have built traction by holding more lavish affairs. This was the case with Enservio, a company that sells expensive software to insurance companies. Enservio was struggling to reach top executives in the insurance industry through other traction channels.

To get traction through offline events, Enservio went all out to organize the Claims Innovation Summit. They held it at the Ritz-Carlton in beautiful Dove Mountain, Arizona, for multiple days. They made sure the event didn't feel like a sales pitch for their services. Instead, they pulled in prominent figures from major consulting firms, respected individuals in the insurance industry, and founders of hot startups to come speak. They then used this group of speakers to attract the industry executives who were their prospective customers. Not only could the executives learn from the speakers, but they could network and vacation at the same time.

The event successfully attracted top decision makers and established Enservio as an industry leader overnight. It has now established this conference as an annual event in its industry.

MicroConf is a smaller conference for self-funded startups that attracts hundreds of founders and sells out in days. It is run by Rob Walling of HitTail. When Rob first started MicroConf he had difficulty attracting people to a conference they'd never heard of. As he said:

> We struggled to sell tickets [for the first MicroConf]. . . . I ran Facebook ads and did [Google] AdWords, but neither really worked. Anything that wasn't relational, where people hadn't heard of the conference, didn't get traction. . . . We also put together an e-book with quotes and articles from some of MicroConf's speakers where you had to pay with a tweet to get it. It went pretty viral, but didn't sell any tickets.
>
> Some people said it was too expensive. I think for some people that was an issue, but I think it comes down to being able to prove value. Since it was unproven, they just didn't know if they were going to spend that $500, plus airfare and hotel, and it would just be a crappy or mediocre conference. Once the first year proved itself, suddenly people were saying we need to raise the price—people have no issue with the price now.

Rob spoke about the types of companies that have the potential to benefit from meetups and other offline events:

> Companies with customers who have shared interests, who have a kind of community or at least a need for one, I think

that's the type of company that will benefit most. I don't know that HitTail would be a good example of a company that could throw a good conference. . . . Our customers are all over the board (real estate, doctors, startups, etc.), so throwing an SEO conference probably wouldn't be all that helpful.

Any niche where the market is online and easily reachable would be a good one, because everyone wants to go to a conference. Any niche where you have recognizable names you can go after would also be good.

Instead of a conference, you may choose to connect with a target group of customers at a meetup. For example, if you're a small SEO software company, you might hold a meetup where you discuss the latest and greatest SEO tactics.

Small meetup groups are more effective than you might expect, especially in the early stages. Seth Godin used meetups when launching his book *Linchpin*. He organized *Linchpin* meetups in cities all across the country through his blog. In total, more than ten thousand people attended these events, where they connected over ideas that Seth wrote about as well as built relationships with one another.

Great meetups can create lasting community connections. The meetup groups that watched the live stream of the first Lean Startup conference continue to meet years afterward: more than twenty cities still have regular "Lean Startup Circle" meetups. These events allow practitioners to continue to connect over the ideas in Eric's book. They've also helped keep his book on the bestseller list.

You can start your own meetup, join an existing one, or even sponsor an event where your prospective customers will be. Meetup.com is the most popular site for doing so.

Nick Pinkston, founder of automated manufacturing startup Plethora Labs and the Hardware Startup Meetup group, saw a need for a community around the budding hardware startup movement. In the Bay Area there were hundreds of events and meetups focused on software startups, but not a single one focused on the unique needs and challenges of hardware startups.

Nick organized his first meetup at TechShop SF. The first meeting drew 60 people and the only expense was $70 for pizza. An event like this makes for a great test case given how easy it is to pull off. In Nick's case, there was lots of interest from attendees—the group now has more than 2,600 members.

Believe it or not, throwing a party can also be an effective way to get some traction. Evite did this when it put on one of the largest parties in the Bay Area for Internet celebrity Mahir Çağri.

Evite was of course responsible for organizing and sending out all invitations. This event exposed Evite to its target customer in a memorable manner. Who doesn't want a party invite? Attendees were then likely to use Evite when throwing their own parties.

Yelp had a similar experience when trying to jump-start usage in new cities. It would throw parties where Yelp Elites (the company's term for top Yelp users) were allowed to RSVP first, given free food and merchandise, and treated as VIPs. When other users heard about such perks, it gave them an incentive to be more active on the site.

OFFLINE EVENT TACTICS

Although MicroConf has become a huge event, Rob suggested that a day-long mini-conference could be a great way for a smaller startup to get traction. It can also be an easy and cheap way to test if there's any interest among your audience for a larger event.

For example, you can select a topic relevant to your product and invite the founders of three local companies to come give short talks on the subject. You could also feature these founders on a panel about a particular topic. You might even take the "unconference" approach and have attendees suggest topics for roundtable discussion, and then allow them to vote on which discussions will take place.

A local university lecture hall is a good place to hold an event like this. Often, universities are willing to open their facilities if it's for an educational purpose and if some of their faculty or students are participating. This type of mini-conference can be done for less than $500.

If your first event is a success, consider scaling up to larger events. The logistics of planning a larger event will take a lot more effort because you need more of everything. Sponsors may be interested in helping you cover the cost of the event. For MicroConf, companies with products built for startups offset the cost of putting on the conference.

Rob also made a few key points about creating a great event. Keeping attendee quality as high as possible is crucial so that those who attend the conference will learn a great deal both from the speakers and from other audience members. Rob has found the best way to do this is to make the ticket price relatively high, so that individuals with successful businesses are more likely to attend than those just starting out.

The structure of an event also plays a critical role in whether the experience works for you and the attendees. With MicroConf, Rob intentionally keeps it small so that attendees have a chance to meet everyone else at the event and the speakers can get to know the attendees. At larger events, speakers get mobbed after they give a talk or sit on a panel. At smaller events, each attendee can connect with every speaker personally. Rob facilitated these conversations by having the speakers sit with the attendees at lunch and participate in roundtable discussions.

If you are creative and willing to try something different, throwing a successful event can be a big win. One of the reasons offline events are effective is that so few startups are doing them. As Rob said:

> *I think the overarching thing for marketing is [startups] need to try more things, and fail faster and more quickly. . . . Trying all of this stuff and seeing what works is paramount. The tried and true approaches like Facebook and AdWords are so crowded now.*
>
> *People need to think about doing things that don't scale. Early on when you're trying to get those first one thousand customers, you have to do things that don't scale. You have to take more risks.*

You can still build a business without being creative. If you don't have creativity, you need money. You need one or the other.

TARGETS

- **Launch at a conference.** Conferences are the biggest and most popular type of offline event. Launching at a conference has been a successful phase I conference tactic. If there isn't a conference that directly brings together your target customers, consider creating one.
- **Test this channel first.** Attend a couple conferences or host a few smaller meetups or a one-day mini-conference.
- **Throw a party.** Having meetups or parties, either alongside conferences or across many cities, is another successful strategy to attract and reward prospective customers.

CHAPTER TWENTY-THREE
Speaking Engagements

In the previous two chapters, we touched on speaking at trade shows and offline events. In this chapter, we will discuss how to land these speaking engagements and how to make them compelling.

It's relatively easy to get started in this channel. Start by giving free talks to small groups of potential customers or partners. Speaking at small events can improve your speaking ability, give you some early traction, and spread your story or message. It's also good for personal growth if you've never done it before: Mark Zuckerberg has talked about how improving at public speaking has vastly improved his management ability. We recommend trying to give at least one talk even if you choose not to pursue this traction channel.

Dan Martell is the founder of Clarity, an advice platform that connects founders with successful entrepreneurs. He spoke to us about getting traction through speaking engagements:

Speaking is funny. You know to me, it's the old-school concept that teaching sells. . . . Teaching is what content marketing is all about: webinars, blog posts, and the like. I look at [these] things as the future of good marketing. The opportunity to teach and be in front of a room for forty-five minutes introducing your company and your story to potential customers is time well spent.

This channel works well wherever there is a group of people in a room that—if you pitched them right—would move the needle for your business. This happens to occur more with enterprise and B2B businesses because they're often at expensive conferences, though Dan has gotten traction from talks he's given for Clarity (a consumer-focused platform).

SPEAKING ENGAGEMENT STRATEGY

You have to get the attention of event organizers to land speaking engagements. Event organizers *need* to fill time at their events. If you have a good idea for a talk and see an event that aligns with an area of your expertise, simply pitch your talk to the event organizers. If your ideas are solid, they will want you. This process becomes even easier as you become a recognized expert.

Steve Barsh, a serial entrepreneur and former CEO of PackLate, has successfully pitched conference organizers to present many times. Rather than pitch them directly on what he wants to talk about, he contacts them and asks them about the ideal topics they want to have speakers cover at an event. Once that is known, he then crafts the perfect pitch: one that hits on key points the organizers want to cover.

To determine where you want to speak, make a list of the events in your industry. Different kinds of events have different crowds and different expectations of speakers. There are a few types of events you should be aware of:

- Premier events are well regarded and attended national or international shows. Often, there will be only a few of these per year in an industry. These events will require much longer lead times to submit a proposal, often six to twelve months.

- Regional events bring together industry players within a day's drive. Depending on the event, expect to land a speaking engagement roughly two to four months before the show.
- Local events draw city residents around a particular topic. As with regional shows, lead times can vary but are usually one to three months before the event.

Organizers consider timing, topic, and credibility when selecting a speaker. By establishing yourself as an expert on an appropriate topic and submitting proposals far in advance, you maximize your chances of securing one of the best speaking engagements at the target show.

Landing speaking engagements is *far* easier if you have expert credentials. After all, if you don't "earn the right" to be onstage, the audience won't give you the attention you deserve. For example, if you run a popular blog, it becomes much easier for organizers and attendees to find and recognize your expertise.

In addition to industry experience, conference organizers will want to see that you are a decent speaker. If you're not well known as a speaker, they'll be hesitant to book you, even for free.

Getting valuable early speaking experience is not difficult. Start by speaking for free at coworking spaces, nonprofits, and smaller conferences or events. Use these smaller-scale appearances to refine your talks and build your speaking reputation.

The world of event organizers is relatively small, and they pay special attention to who is speaking at events. As a result, you'll find your number of engagements growing organically. As Dan told us:

> *To become a speaker you have to speak once. If you speak and you're good, people in the audience will ask you to speak at other events. That's just how it happens. I've never marketed myself as a speaker; it's not in my bio or anything. What*

happens is, you speak at a conference, people see it or talk
about it, and you get invited to other ones.

If you do a good job at smaller events, you can leverage them into talks at larger ones by asking for referrals and using past events as social proof.

SPEAKING ENGAGEMENT TACTICS

When you start a talk, the audience is usually thinking about two questions: *Why are you important enough to be the one giving a talk? What value can you offer me?* These questions will be burning in their minds until you address them, so answer them immediately. For this reason, Dan told us he does his own introductions and highlights how he started and sold his two previous companies (Flowtown and Spheric) for millions.

Once you've captured the audience's attention, keep it with a gripping story. All successful talks tell a story. Your story is about *what* your startup is doing, *why* you're doing it, and specifically *how* you got to where you are or *where* things are going.

Of course, we have only so many captivating stories. That's why Dan gives the same one or two core talks, only slightly modifying each to fit the audience. He never does custom talks and always reuses his slides, so his speaking engagements are always well rehearsed and received:

> *I usually figure out who are two target customers that I want*
> *to reach, because it's hard to give more than two good talks.*
> *For Clarity, it's entrepreneurs and potential partners. Try to*
> *figure out the two tracks your potential customers might be*
> *interested in and try to teach them about that. For us, it's*
> *helping entrepreneurs get great advice and how it's changed*
> *my life, so I have a talk about my entrepreneurial journey*
> *and why getting the right advice can change your life.*

Giving a limited number of talks is helpful in another way: it gives you more practice per talk, which helps you identify spots that may not be clicking with the audience. The more practiced and comfortable you are, the better your talks will be and the more you can improve them.

If you want to focus on speaking engagements, we spoke with Dan about a few more advanced tactics you can use.

Record your speaking engagements. If you're at an event of 250 people and you've just given your best speech ever, you've still reached only 250 people. However, if you can record your best speech ever, then you can post clips, thereby exposing your story to thousands of people who would never have seen it otherwise. Among this group of online viewers will be conference organizers who will book you for future events.

Leveraging social media to reach people *outside* of the conference is a similar tactic. Rand Fishkin of Moz tweets his slides before every presentation, which lets his followers find out what he'll be talking about. Then, when he posts a video of his talk, there is already some buzz and interest in watching and sharing it.

Dan Martell will even try to leverage social media *during* his talk. He asks for the audience's "divided attention," meaning he wants them to tweet and share good content from his presentation as he gives it. To facilitate this, he includes his Twitter handle on every slide and asks people to tweet at him if they really identified with something he said. This way, he can find out the content his audience enjoyed the most, while also growing his reach.

On top of asking his audience to tweet and text, Dan also gives the audience a call to action at the end of his presentations. This is a simple request of the audience—something like asking them to sign up to a mailing list or to check out a link where they can see his slides. This tactic tells him whether or not members of the audience found the information engaging enough to act on it.

We already mentioned that Dan prepares only two talks that he delivers at speaking engagements. But what if one conference asks for a twenty-minute presentation and another asks for sixty? It's time-consuming to prepare a whole new talk: it's more efficient to tailor your existing slides to a specific audience or event. As Dan said:

The best talks I've ever seen are where each slide is essentially a seven-minute story with a beginning, middle, and end. Once you get good at that, and you have these canned slides, you can change a sixty-minute talk to a twenty-minute talk just by taking slides out.

The slides for your presentation are an important part of any talk you'll give. Every slide in your presentation should be engaging.

As we mentioned early on, the main driver for being a speaker in the first place is to build relationships. At most conferences there is a speakers' dinner, where presenters get to meet one another and network. If there isn't one scheduled, Dan usually takes the liberty of scheduling one.

Similar to trade shows, you can also do preparation ahead of time based upon who is likely to attend the event where you are speaking. Get a list of attendees from event organizers and contact people you would like to meet. Tell them exactly when and where you are speaking, and suggest meeting up afterward. Now that they've heard you talk they'll be much more receptive to your pitch.

Speaking engagements are one of the few traction channels that can quickly cement your place in an industry. If you give the right talk at the right time to the right people, it can make you a respected industry leader overnight.

TARGETS

- **Remember that you are doing organizers a favor by presenting.** Event organizers *need* to fill time at their events.
- **Submit authoritative proposals far in advance.** Organizers consider timing, topic, and credibility when selecting a speaker. By establishing yourself as an expert on the right topic and submitting proposals far in advance, you maximize your chances of securing one of the best speaking engagements at the target show.

- **Tell a story onstage.** Without a story, the audience will lose interest. We suggest telling a story about *why* you're doing what you're doing, and specifically present insights only you can give through your unique position as a startup founder. Make it exciting!

CHAPTER TWENTY-FOUR
Community Building

Community building involves investing in the connections among your customers, fostering those relationships and helping them bring more people into your startup's circle. We interviewed the founders of reddit, Wikipedia, Stack Exchange, *Startup Digest*, and Quibb to tell us how they created, grew, and nurtured their communities.

You probably know people who won't stop talking about how helpful Yelp is for choosing a restaurant and about the reviews they've submitted. These people are known as community evangelists—passionate customers who tell others about how awesome a product is.

Maybe after hearing about Yelp from your friend for a third time, you used the app yourself when looking for a dinner spot on Saturday night. Then you found it so useful that you too became a Yelp evangelist. You started leaving reviews and telling people about them. That's how evangelists spread the word about a product and help build its community further.

COMMUNITY BUILDING STRATEGY

Every individual we interviewed emphasized how helpful it was to have an existing audience to jump-start their community-building efforts. For example, Wikipedia began with a small group of users from the Nupedia user group (an earlier online encyclopedia project).

Stack Exchange is a network of high-quality question-and-answer sites, the most famous being Stack Overflow. Joel Spolsky and Jeff Atwood founded the company in 2008. Both were already Internet famous: Joel as the founder of Fog Creek Software, and Jeff as a writer at codinghorror.com.

Thanks to their well-trafficked blogs, Jeff and Joel presented their ideas for Stack Overflow to readers who gave them feedback before the site launched. They even had the community vote on the *name* for Stack Overflow, and received nearly seven thousand submissions!

While this illustrates the power of an existing audience, it is an atypical startup experience. Few startups manage to get seven thousand customers after six months, much less seven thousand votes on the name of a site that doesn't even exist. However, having an audience is not a prerequisite for building a successful community.

Chris McCann started *Startup Digest* by emailing twenty-two friends in the Bay Area about local tech events. To grow the list more, Chris started giving twenty-second *Startup Digest* pitches at events he attended. His pitches proved effective: membership grew into the low thousands in a matter of months. Today there are more than 250,000 members of the *Startup Digest* community, and it all started with those twenty-two friends and bootstrapping off local startup meetups.

People want to feel like they're part of something bigger than themselves. You need to have a mission if you want to build an awesome community. A powerful mission gives your community a shared sense of purpose and motivates them to contribute. As Jeff Atwood said:

> *We had a manifesto, and an idea of what we wanted to accomplish. And people bought into the vision because it was*

about them being awesome. . . . [It is] about creating some-thing that helps everyone in material and specific ways. It helps you get better at your job, at something you love doing. There was an idealism that people bought into with Stack Exchange, and we were out there talking about it all that time.

Being open with your community is the best way to get them to buy into your mission. Jeff and Joel solicited feedback every step of the way, and built the site their community wanted. When Stack Overflow launched, their audience was already excited and had shaped the direction of the site. This resulted in hundreds of customers in the first days, and thousands during the first month.

From our interviews we also discovered that it's *critical* to foster connections among your community (through forums, events, and user groups). When you encourage your customers to connect around your startup, they feel more cohesive as a community and can come up with ideas that you may not think of yourself. Jeff said that failing to initially allow cross-connections was his biggest mistake in building Stack Overflow:

When people ask me what our biggest mistake was in build-ing Stack Overflow I'm glad I don't have to fudge around with platitudes. I can honestly and openly point to a huge, honking, ridiculously dumb mistake I made from the very first day of development on Stack Overflow. . . . I didn't see the need for a Meta.

Meta is, of course, the place where you go to discuss the place. Take a moment and think about what that means. Meta is for people who care so deeply about their community that they're willing to go one step further, to come together and spend even more of their time deciding how to maintain and govern it. So, in a nutshell, I was telling the people who loved Stack Overflow the most of all to basically . . . f**k off and go away.

Community members love to hear from other members. But they would also love to hear from *you*. You will want to connect with your evangelists and let them know that you value them.

In reddit's early days, any individual who wrote about reddit would get an email from cofounder Alexis Ohanian thanking them. Alexis also sent shirts, stickers, and other gifts to early users. He went so far as to coordinate an open bar tour for redditors, where redditors connected and drank on reddit's dime.

Sending emails and gifts is great, but nothing beats personal interaction. It's just easier to form a lasting relationship with someone when you're sharing a laugh, a meal, or a drink. In that way, community building works nicely with other channels like offline events and speaking engagements. These occasions present great opportunities for customers to connect with you and with one another.

A challenge with community building as you scale is keeping its quality high. The meaning of quality depends on the service the startup provides. For Yelp, it might be the accuracy of its reviews; Wikipedia, the usefulness of its articles; reddit, the relevance of its links and comments.

Stack Overflow wanted to create the best question-and-answer site for developers—a community that truly helped developers get better at their jobs. Upon launch, Jeff established strict guidelines (decided on in tandem with the community) so that only practical, answerable questions would be allowed. Then he placed these guidelines on the Stack Overflow FAQ.

Because these community guidelines were prominently featured on the site, users often policed the site on their own—even more aggressively than Jeff himself would have. Not only did this keep quality high, but it kept members of the community engaged and invested in the future of the site.

Everyone we talked to about community building emphasized the importance of maintaining community quality. Wikipedia developed strict guidelines for everything from the types of articles to include on the site to how conflicts of interest should be handled. *Startup Digest* focused on content selected by community members in each of its cities. Quibb uses an invite-only model to recruit people they feel would be a positive addition to their community. Like Stack Overflow, reddit developed a karma system based on voting that determines what links and comments are displayed prominently.

Unfortunately, a common occurrence is that the quality of communities starts out strong but gets diluted over time as evangelists either leave or get drowned out by newer community members. This decline in the overall quality of the community causes more good people to leave, which creates a downward spiral from which many communities don't recover. To prevent this negative cycle, it is important to focus on quality early on and set standards that can be maintained as the community grows.

When quality remains high, many communities become an essential asset for the managing company or organization. Consider Wikipedia: Its goal is to compile the world's knowledge in one place. To reach this goal, it has built the largest group of knowledge contributors and editors ever assembled.

Other startups like Yelp and Codecademy have built core groups of customers to accomplish their company goals. Yelp would be nothing without restaurant reviews from its users; many of Codecademy's programming lessons are user generated as well. Both sites have worked to attract people to their vision (Yelp's to allow people to discover their neighborhoods; Codecademy's to teach the world to code), and have thrived by leveraging their users to help accomplish that vision.

Like building an asset, your customers can also help you develop your actual product. Not only does this kind of community improve your product, but they will love you for giving them the chance to help.

For software companies, their code is the product. Some companies open-source their code, making it freely available for anyone to use, modify, or improve. Tom Preston-Werner, founder of popular code hosting site GitHub, points out that open-sourcing code generates free advertising and a lot of goodwill. GitHub is beloved by developers everywhere because it allows anyone working on an open source project to use GitHub free of charge. This drove a lot of its early adoption: when a developer wanted to work on a side project, GitHub was the first place that came to mind.

Another use of community is for hiring. Everyone working at Gabriel's startup DuckDuckGo was a member of the DuckDuckGo community first.

Hires that come from your community already buy into your mission. These are people you really want on your team—community members who didn't just believe in your mission, but also took the initiative to help you achieve it.

Chris McCann (of *Startup Digest*) talked about the types of companies that will benefit from community building:

> *I think building a community can be your traction. This is no small thing: it can truly get to crazy proportions on its own. That being said, there are definitely products and services that don't lend themselves to community building. If I were doing something with advertising and retargeting, it might be hard to build a community around that.*
>
> *There are some businesses that lend themselves to doing this very well. Companies whose core function is the connecting of people are best set up to take advantage of community. Whether that's a trade show thing, an investment thing, whatever: when a company's underlying value is in bringing people together, and where people matter in the system, that's where this community stuff can really take off.*

TARGETS

- **Cultivate and empower evangelists.** Foster cross-connection among them and among community members in general.
- **Set high standards from the start.** Focus on community quality early on and set strict standards that can be maintained as the community grows. You can build tools and processes into your community to help your community police itself.
- **Bootstrap off an existing audience.** Find initial evangelists by sharing your mission with complementary communities online and at offline events.

ACKNOWLEDGMENTS

First, we want to thank everyone who shared their traction stories and tips with us. Without you this book would not be possible:

Jimmy Wales, Cofounder of Wikipedia

Alexis Ohanian, Cofounder of reddit

Eric Ries, Author of *The Lean Startup*

Rand Fishkin, Founder of Moz

Noah Kagan, Founder of AppSumo

Patrick McKenzie, CEO of Bingo Card Creator

Sam Yagan, Cofounder of OkCupid

Andrew Chen, Investor in 500 Startups

Dharmesh Shah, Founder of HubSpot

ACKNOWLEDGMENTS

Justin Kan, Founder of Justin.tv

Mark Cramer, CEO of Surf Canyon

Colin Nederkoorn, CEO of Customer.io

Jason Cohen, Founder of WP Engine

Chris Fralic, Partner at First Round Capital

Paul English, CEO of Kayak

Rob Walling, Founder of MicroConf

Brian Riley, Cofounder of SureStop

Steve Welch, Cofounder of DreamIt

Jason Kincaid, Blogger at *TechCrunch*

Nikhil Sethi, Founder of Adaptly

Rick Perreault, CEO of Unbounce

Alex Pachikov, Evernote Founding Team

David Skok, Partner at Matrix

Ashish Kundra, CEO of myZamana

David Hauser, Founder of Grasshopper

Matt Monahan, CEO of Inflection

Jeff Atwood, Cofounder of Discourse

Dan Martell, CEO of Clarity

Chris McCann, Founder of *Startup Digest*

Ryan Holiday, Exec at American Apparel

Todd Vollmer, Enterprise Sales Veteran

Sandi MacPherson, Founder of Quibb

ACKNOWLEDGMENTS

Andrew Warner, Founder of Mixergy

Sean Murphy, Founder of SKMurphy

Satish Dharmaraj, Partner at Redpoint Ventures

Garry Tan, Partner at Y Combinator

Steve Barsh, CEO of PackLate

Michael Bodekaer, Cofounder of Smartlaunch

Each of you played a critical role in shaping this book and making it a useful resource. We apologize if we left anyone off this list.

We'd also like to thank our early readers for their helpful comments and feedback, as well as Eric Nelson, Michael Zakhar, and Brian Spadora for their editing help. Additional thanks to Eve Weinberg for pulling together our initial cover and Chris Morast and Doug Brown for producing a beautiful Web site and book.

To Andrew Warner of Mixergy: your introductions and help throughout the whole process set the tone for the book and gave us momentum and a plan in the early days when we were just starting to tackle this project.

To all the founders, investors, and others who have published blog posts, resources, and other tips that we've used in this book, thank you. We hope this book helps you in the same way your resources have helped us.

On a personal note (from Justin), thank you to my parents Kim and Peter Mares for your support and love throughout this process. Without you this book never would have happened.

Similarly (from Gabriel), thank you to my wife, Lauren, and the superhero kids, Eli and Ryan.

If you found this book useful, please spread the word. Tell your friends. Leave an Amazon review. Every little bit helps!

APPENDIX: MIDDLE RING TESTS

Below are some basic middle ring traction tests to get you started in each traction channel. These tests are designed for phase I startups. As explained earlier, middle ring tests in phase I should cost less than a thousand dollars and take less than one month of time. However, please keep in mind that these may not be the best tests for you to run. You might come up with better tests in your Bullseye process.

Targeting Blogs—Contact ten niche blogs and try to get them to review your product. To make it really easy for them, offer to walk them through the product (in person if you can find local bloggers or connect with them at events). You can also make the offer even more enticing by giving them the opportunity to give something away to their audience (discounts, T-shirt contest, etc.). Alternatively, you could find blogs that don't run advertisements and ask several if you could run an advertisement on them for $100/month.

Publicity—Contact five relevant local reporters about your company and try to get them to write about you. Local stories are much easier to get written since there is already local interest. Offer to meet them in person to walk through the product. Their phone numbers might be listed on their publication Web sites. Otherwise, try reaching out on Twitter or at events you know they'll be covering.

Unconventional PR—Host a contest around your product. This contest could be as simple as a cash giveaway for creative product usage or as complicated as a game constructed around your product. Once it's set up, try a bit of both paid media (e.g., Twitter ads) and earned media (e.g., local press and blogs) to promote your contest. Alternatively, try a more creative approach with an infographic or video you think could go viral with your audience. If you have a large incumbent competitor, it could be explaining how they do something poorly in some way (and at the end how you do it better).

Search Engine Marketing—Try four ads in Bing Ads (often cheaper than Google AdWords). These ads should be on keywords you're highly confident will convert into long-term customers. Try some of these keywords even if they seem relatively expensive compared with keywords you're less confident about. You want to figure out in the best-case conversion scenario whether SEM could work. Make sure before you turn them on that you have everything set up correctly to actually detect conversions (and not just clicks to your site). If you can't automate that, then you can ask new customers how they heard of you (manually if necessary).

Social and Display Ads—Try a Facebook or Twitter ad campaign. Use their targeting capabilities to target two niche audiences that you think would really convert well. You can get very specific here, and you should. On Twitter, advertise against Twitter handles you think are directly related to your product (like industry leaders, aggregators, or even competitors). For Facebook, advertise against complementary affinity groups. If there are local areas you have a hunch would work better, for example, certain cities, then restrict your ads further to those areas. Make sure you try a few different images in your ads, as the image can have a major effect on performance.

Offline Ads—Advertise on a niche podcast. With these advertisements, the host usually reads your copy directly to his listeners. It needs to be niche enough where you think the audience would really like your offer, but still small enough where it is reasonably priced (as podcast ads can get expensive for larger audiences). Alternatively, run a few ads in local papers.

Search Engine Optimization—Test a long-tail SEO strategy by making some content-rich pages. Perhaps your product can naturally produce data for these pages, or maybe you have enough data from making and researching your product. Link to these new pages right from your home page (e.g., on the footer), as that will give them the highest rankings. Let relevant people know about your content and see if they'll repost it with a link back to the original source. Alternatively, test a fat-head SEO strategy by identifying promising fat-head keywords and then running search engine ads to see how effective the traffic may be. This is a very similar basic test to Search Engine Marketing itself, though the keywords may be different.

Content Marketing—Start a company blog and write one blog post a week for a month. Promote your posts on Twitter and on link-sharing sites (e.g., reddit). If you see any significant audience growth and conversion, double down and commit to a few more months. Turn on comments for your posts and engage with any commenters. Try to write controversial or surprising posts, ideally using new data you've researched. Alternatively, do a couple of guest posts on other blogs.

Email Marketing—Contact ten email newsletters in your niche and advertise on at least two of them where it makes sense financially. If they don't usually run advertisements in their emails, ask to sponsor the list for a week or month. Alternatively, develop a seven-email mini-course, where you teach something relevant to your product. Make a landing page for the course and drive some traffic to it. At the end of the mini-course, upsell prospective customers to becoming real customers of your product.

Viral Marketing—Build a viral loop into your product and measure your viral coefficient and viral cycle time. See which step is the weakest in your viral loop (signup percentage, number of invites, click-through percentage). Run five tests to improve this weakest step and see how it affects your viral coefficient. If it gets near 0.5, then you might be on to something.

Engineering as Marketing—Make a simple, free tool tangentially relevant to your company; for example, a calculator of some kind that would be useful to prospective customers. Put it on its own domain and name it something that people would search for. Collect contact information in exchange for using the tool. Reach out to anyone who uses your tool with a personal email about your main product.

Business Development—Write down three types of companies that could be useful to yours in terms of partnerships. For example, are there companies with complementary products? Identify some smaller players and reach out to two in each category, six in total. Have conversations with as many as will have them to gauge interest. Try to strike at least one deal.

Sales—List twenty local, prospective customers. Try to get warm intros to as many as possible and meet with them in person to discuss your product. Use the SPIN approach we presented in the Sales chapter. Alternatively, reach out cold over email to one hundred prospective customers who you think have a high likelihood of converting into real customers.

Affiliate Programs—Register your product at the most relevant major affiliate network (there is a list at the end of the Affiliate Programs chapter). Recruit twenty affiliates from this program using a simple and attractive payout structure. Contact each affiliate personally to walk them through the product, which will greatly increase the chances they will sell effectively. Alternatively, contact existing customers you think might be well connected to prospective customers and strike affiliate deals with them.

Existing Platforms—Identify the most relevant niche platform where your audience hangs out online (e.g., Craigslist, Tumblr, etc.). Research the best practices for promoting products on that platform and then do so with your product. Try some paid tools or advertising if available for the platform. Alternatively, make a simple browser extension and try to get featured.

Trade Shows—Follow the procedure outlined in the Trade Shows chapter to list all the obviously relevant events over the next year. Dig deeper on the next few months to make sure smaller events are on your list. Ask your local startup community if anyone has been to these events.

Exhibit at the one that seems most promising. Alternatively, go to a bigger event as an attendee.

Offline Events—Put together a one-day mini-conference. Pull together a few regional speakers to speak during the day. Host it at a university, and leverage its resources. You may need to make a professor one of the speakers to make it work. Alternatively, sponsor several local events and ask to speak for a few minutes about what you're working on at the beginning of the events.

Speaking Engagements—Contact three local meetup group organizers relevant to your product and ask if you can speak at an upcoming event. Present your company in the context of your personal story. How did you come to be where you are today? How are you uniquely solving a problem with your product? What are your ambitious plans? Alternatively, pitch a talk at a regional conference.

Community Building—Join three online forums where your customers hang out and engage on at least twenty threads on each. Do this over a month so you don't look spammy. Similarly, don't just plug your product directly; truly engage as a useful member of the community. Include references to your product where appropriate and in your signature. Alternatively, start putting together your own community using an online forum tool.

INDEX

INDEX

INDEX

INDEX

viral pockets, 126, 128
Virgin Galactic, 57–58
Visual Website Optimizer, 29, 70
Vollmer, Todd, 151
Volpe, Mike, 100

Walling, Rob, 7, 186–87, 188–89
Wall Street, 52
Walmart, 82, 160
Warby Parker, 79
Washington Post, 48, 142, 144–45
Weebly, 120
Wendy's, 89
WePay, 58–59
WhatsApp, 120
widgets, 99, 129, 133
Wikipedia, 7, 98, 199, 201
Williams, Evan, 184–85

Wilson, Fred, 106
Winfrey, Oprah, 50
word of mouth, 120, 127
WordPress, 114, 131
WP Engine, 4, 113–14, 131, 175
writer's block, 105

Yagan, Sam, 5, 103, 104–5
Yahoo!, 137–38
Y Combinator, 2
yellow pages, ads in, 86
Yelp, 98, 184, 188, 198, 201, 202
YouTube, 4, 44, 46, 59, 81, 120–21, 170

Zappos, 61, 159, 160
Zuckerberg, Mark, 191
Zynga, 31